Spiritual
BUSINESS

Also by Michael Peter Langevin
Secrets of the Ancient Incas

Spiritual BUSINESS

The Amazing and
True Story of
Magical Blend
Magazine

MICHAEL PETER LANGEVIN

HAMPTON ROADS
PUBLISHING COMPANY, INC.

Hampton Roads Publishing Company, Inc.
1125 Stoney Ridge Road
Charlottesville, VA 22902

434-296-2772
fax: 434-296-5096
e-mail: hrpc@hrpub.com
www.hrpub.com

If you are unable to order this book from your local
bookseller, you may order directly from the publisher.
Call 1-800-766-8009, toll-free.

Library of Congress Cataloging-in-Publication Data

Langevin, Michael Peter, 1952-
Spiritual business : the amazing and true story of Magical blend
magazine / Michael Peter Langevin.
    p. cm.
ISBN 1-57174-370-7 (5 1/2 x 8 1/2 tp : alk. paper)
1. Magical blend (San Francisco, CA : 1989)--History 2. Langevin,
Michael Peter, 1952- 3. New Age movement--Periodicals--History. I.
Title.
BP605.N483M2535 2004
299'.93--dc22
                                                2004007803

10 9 8 7 6 5 4 3 2 1

Printed on acid-free paper in the United States

DEDICATION

To all those who have worked on the staff of *Magical Blend* magazine over the past 25 years this book is dedicated, first and foremost. Second, to the journey, the players, and the changing times. This book is dedicated to all the people, places, and things that have touched the birth and life of *Magical Blend* magazine. There are no words that I can write or speak that would express the depth of my heartfelt gratitude. It flows from the very depth of my being. In my mind's eye, as I traveled back in time to write this book, I sat in wonder at my good fortune. It has been my blessing to be touched by so many very special souls. I have attempted to tell *Magical Blend*'s wild history as truthfully as possible, but emphasizing the details that I felt would make the best story.

The ideals and the culture of 25 years ago are not those of the present day. People grow and change, and over time they hold different views on subjects, careers, and life in general. Therefore, I have liberally changed names and certain events so as not to barge into anyone's present space. Twenty-five years is a long time.

I could write a second book much longer than this one, made up of many important people, places, and events that I left out of this one. I just wrote the story that flowed of its own will. Please enjoy.

ACKNOWLEDGMENTS

I would like to first acknowledge my strong and forgiving wife, Deborah Lynn. Without her by my side, I never could have accomplished most of what I have so far in this life. Without all that she does and forgives, I would not have been able to write this or any other book.

Then, I would like to thank the best son a man could ever have, Henry Miguel Langevin. His great attitude and wonderful sense of humor inspire me.

I also have to thank the most amazing daughter a man could have, Sophia Zila Langevin. Her persistence and youthful wisdom have taught me so much.

I would never be able to be me without the constant, unconditional, loving support given me all my life by my Mom, Eileen Winifred Langevin.

Even more than myself, Frank DeMarco turned this book into reality. His quality friendship, advice, and important spiritual work are priceless gifts.

I owe a debt of gratitude to my friend Mike Richman, without whose efforts this book would have made little sense. Mike is an unsung hero and a great editor.

My business partner for 15 of *Magical Blend*'s twenty-five years, Jerry Snider, his hard work, excellent editing, exquisite writing, countless other skills, his vision, adaptability, and friendship were essential in making *Magical Blend* what it was.

The art directors for a key nine and ten years, Mathew Courtway and Yuka Hirota, their ascetics, graphic and design skills, ceaseless hard work, dedication, and friendship defined *Magical Blend* for a many important years. Mathew skillfully designed the Don Juan and Christ covers that grace the cover of this book.

The first cover artist, John Oberdorf, who's first cover also can be seen on this book's cover. His exquisite paintings and his single-minded dedication to them as well as his friendship have inspired me often.

The unofficial first Art Director of *Magical Blend*, Jeff Fletcher, from 1978 to 1988 he contributed in innumerable ways to the first chapters of *Magical Blend Magazine*. A true friend.

To the man who brought *Magical Blend* into the fourth dimension, Mike Ferris; somehow he got edited out of the story, however Mike's contributions were many and his programming the data base 4-D served us thirteen years.

My loving siblings Spider, Dan, Susanne, Pat, Nancy, and Liz have helped and taught me so very much. Few people can be as blessed as I with such strong sibling love and encouragement.

With my Dad's passing, I have grown much closer to my stepsiblings Russ, and Karen and Michael Franchise, for which I am grateful.

I am fortunate to have a wonderful stepmom, Gemma. Her friendship and appreciation are special in my life.

Then there is the memory of my Dad. He wasn't perfect but he became a great friend and advisor and I miss him dearly.

My nephew Rueben dances to a Costa Rican beat. I love that.

My niece Freea, her husband John, and their new daughter Sydney Noel are such a loving family. My niece Ayla Maria is smart and charismatic and will achieve much in her life.

My best friends David Himmer, Richard Daab, and Lottie Hacket have always been special people in my life. Then there's my other great friend, Gene Ketelhohn, whose name I spelled wrong in my last book. And he was the person who turned me on to health food, tai chi, and much more!

Then there are all the *Magical Blend* and MB Media staffs, past, present, and future.

As I write these words, Paul Stevens has been MB Media's C.O.O. for over a year. I hope that we work together in such productive harmony for many more. Paul is the best businessman I have ever worked with and has been essential in our record-setting recent growth.

Rene Schmidt has been *Magical Blend*'s art director and techno shaman for over ten years. He is a true friend and a true genius.

Kathy Hawthorne is leaving our staff once again because her husband Mike is retiring early. I'm happy for them, but sad for us, because Kathy is quite simply the best office manager we have ever had.

Susan Dobra has been our managing editor for over two years. What a creative and big-hearted friend.

Anna Harris is our associate editor. She does a great job in helping to focus and organize all of our writing. Thanks, Anna.

Eric Baland has the honor of being the employee I have fired and rehired most in our history. He is a database prodigy and a nonconformist probably more than anyone who ever worked in our company. And that's saying something.

Izumi Nakatsuka is our best webmaster since we first went online. Randy Schmidt is our eBay and online store creator and prosperity magnet, which is a nice thing to be.

To today's ever evolving advertising sales staff you all know who you are and were. You are almost always challenging and fun people to work with.

To the Inca goddesses and gods: Another piece of our agreement is fulfilled!

To the Spirit who guides and personifies *Magical Blend:* Can you please make it a little easier now?

To all other spiritual entities and forces that have blessed my life and helped to bring about *Magical Blend*'s continued transformations: Thank you.

And to all those people who are so important in my life, many of whom I've never even met—the readers of *Magical Blend*—thank you for being part of our story. Actually, thank you for being the story, the one that we write together each and every day.

CONTENTS

A WORD ABOUT DRUGS

This book is a reflection of my memories of the highlights of how *Magical Blend* grew up, survived, and prospered during its first 25 years. There are many references to drug use, and even abuse, which may seem blasé or even romanticized. I did not avoid them because they were an important element in *Magical Blend*'s evolution. I in no way mean to glorify them or endorse their recreational uses. I have not done drugs for years, with the exception of the occasional prescription given to me by my doctor and the occasional use of Shamanic hallucinatory substances. My children, wife, extended family, and friends are very aware that I had drug abuse problems in my past, and that I hung out and worked with many more people who did.

At more than one point in its history, *Magical Blend* was considered to be in the same genre as *High Times* because we seemed to so thoroughly endorse drug use. That chapter is long finished. I now feel strongly that recreational drug use is dangerous and harmful and should not be indulged in by anyone, anywhere, least of all in the workplace. Even marijuana usually makes people lazy, sloppy, and unambitious, with other personality altering effects.

Yet, though I'm opposed to recreational drug use, I am equally opposed to laws against the possession, sales, or use of any substance. I feel U.S. drug laws are archaic and that no individual should spend a single day in jail for the victimless use of drugs. The U.S. war on drugs has devastated the culturally important cocoa leaf farms of Peru, Bolivia, and Ecuador, and has placed a multitude of U.S. citizens, the majority of whom are African American or Latino, in jails or on probation I feel without just cause.

That being said, ritualistic drug use has great historical and cultural importance, and I feel that natural hallucinogens, used under appropriate shamanic supervision, can widely expand an individual's perspectives, insights, and awareness, allowing them to access dimensions in spirit that later can be returned to in dreams, meditation, undrugged rituals, or prayer.

So please read the drug-related sections of this book with the facts in mind. I feel most drug use is not a good thing, yet neither are laws against their use. Each individual should be able to make their own personal decisions about drugs and anything else which affects only themselves and their lives.

A MAGICAL FUTURE

There is a crossing of energies coming to all living beings on the planet Earth. This shift in mental and spiritual energy will intensify between now and the year 2012, and between now and then every being on Earth will have to make a decision: To either stand up and evolve or to fall back and repeat the cycles of history filled with suffering, ignorance, corrupted leaders, greed, and selfishness.

At the present time, precious few people are aware of the motivations for the decisions that they are making every day and in each moment. Some are deciding to listen to their own, personal, higher guidance. Some are deciding to remain victims. It is beyond the stretch of most human imaginations, but I personally believe that the Earth will actually duplicate itself in the very near future. The higher vibrational energies will form a renewed Earth that will revolve around new energy fields. The lower vibrational energies that are with us now will continue to recycle along the same path that the Earth has taken for the last 250,000 years. This choice, to embrace either our higher or lower vibrations, is one that now confronts us all.

As I was finishing this book, I had a night dream. In it, a me from the future is attempting an untried experiment in time travel. I am attempting to send parts of this manuscript back in time to my present-day self in the year 2004. My memory of that future dream is something like the following:

As I write these words, it is the year 2012. The world has gotten very strange and by all signs it is about to get even stranger. There is an incredible variety of ways of functioning now. Many people have become telepathic. This phenomenon started with increased reports that people could hear each other's thoughts in offices, stores, schools, hospitals, and pretty much everywhere else. It happened more and more until one day it simply exploded all at once. Now it seems as though half the people you meet can either read minds or project their thoughts into other's heads. But this isn't all. Many people report hearing voices from disincarnated beings. Some believe that the voices are of dead relatives or friends, while others think of them as space brothers or the white brotherhood. There are those who feel that they are of our higher divine selves, or even angels or God beginning not only to speak with them, but to actually share their bodies and minds.

The third world has risen up in prosperity and many children who only a decade ago were suffering with dire poverty and hunger are now living in splendor and material wealth. Yet there have been earthquakes, floods, strange weather patterns, wars, and famines in the United States, Canada, Europe, Japan, and the rest of the previously developed world. These nations have pretty much taken on the role of suffering that the third world once endured. The death, disease, destruction, and population migrations that brought all this about would be unimaginable to you in your comfortable and predictable world. It didn't matter the color of your skin, your politics, your religion, or even what college you or your parents went to. When the changes began they were unexpected and unpredictable. They rippled across borders and socioeconomic separations as water flows down a hill. Most everyone was uprooted and ruined financially, and many suffered far worse. But in disaster also comes opportunity. A great number of resourceful, formerly poor, people became millionaires overnight. Most of the advances in technology have come in the areas of disaster and disease prevention and cure. Nanotech transporters, food replicators, and time travel devices are starting to be invented, or I guess you could say have just arrived from the realms of science fiction to reality.

The very way humans view and interface with the material world is beginning to alter greatly. Our understanding and interactions with nature are becoming so much more environmentally reconnection oriented. Our financial, educational, and political systems are evolving and becoming more enlightened each passing day. Poetry, music, mathematics, art, and words can only hint, at their best, at what expanded reality is. To describe it, to capture it, is to lessen it. Each moment and experience is magically unique.

The undeniable nature of spirit is the very essence of our universe; it is almost beyond the human mind to fully grasp for it is beyond limit. Human's are beginning to realize and explore the fact that we have the potential to create and enter almost any reality they can imagine, for we are so much more powerful than we dared hope, and the universe contains all possibilities. Yet this information has been hidden from us till now. As it is revealed and shared, the miracles of our existence are all awaiting those who read this and persist. Each of you must believe in a better you and a better future, and work however you can to get here.

I'm attempting to send this message back in time because time itself seems to be altering. Perhaps it is becoming more permeable to us here in 2012. I want to take advantage of this permeability to warn people of Earth's approaching cosmic crossroad.

So, people, please read this small story. Stretch your imagination, get out of your lazy rut, and turn aside self-ishness. By my estimation, there is precious little time before these cataclysmic changes begin to unfold. Use the comfortable predictability of your current world to make the proper choices that will bring about the New Earth. Reconsider your life choices in the context of what will best bring about the golden age of humanity.

OK, by now you probably hope that I just have an overactive imagination. That would be an easy explanation for my often bizarre self. Still, you have to admit that this is an interesting dream to have as I am finishing writing this book. What do you think?

I am a man who has had visions, spoken to Gods, and enjoyed wonderful friendships with shamans, magicians, and gifted psychics. Yet I don't know for certain what the future holds for me or *Magical Blend*, the magazine that I founded and have operated for the past 25 years. Of course, in my heart of hearts, I see *Magical Blend* as the catalyst of the coming shifts in consciousness described above. I feel fortunate that we are still here to help people deal with the repercussions of these changes. There have been many times over the past couple of decades when our survival was far from certain. But I am convinced that beings who first spoke to me long ago in Vera Cruz, as well as the entire pantheon of Incan deities, have been watching over our endeavor and helping us not only to survive, but to thrive. I believe that the reason for this is that we have a large role to play in assisting humanity in the years to come.

Even with the guidance and support of mystical beings, I don't know if *Magical Blend* would have made it if we had not transformed ourselves from a patchwork group with high ideals but little experience to a professional, hardworking, and mature organization. All of this required adaptability on everyone's part. To be honest, I still have a difficult time spelling or even pronouncing the word "capitalist."

In high school and college, my intention was to become a guerrilla fighter who dedicated his life to tearing down evil economic systems based on capitalism and freeing people held captive by corporate greed and political chicanery. Or, at least, I wanted to be an undercover diplomat following the same agenda. I considered myself to be a communist, or at least a socialist. I hated money, the capitalist system, and all that they stood for. It seemed to me that these things were dehumanizing and those who followed their principles only wanted to ruin the environment and break the spirits of the people.

Life has a funny way of making you into what you hate. I have owned and operated a business for over 25 years. I have had to heal many of my own misconceptions. The main one is that money is not evil, nor does it necessarily corrupt. Money is only a tool, like a knife or fire, which can be used to inflict pain or to bring about healing. I now believe that if a person follows their heart, that wealth, recognition, and influence will flow to them as they desire it and can use it wisely and efficiently.

Although this sums up my philosophy fairly well, I have also found wishful thinking and good intentions are not enough.

Magical Blend has made me into a businessman so that it could survive and serve more people better. In 1979, I thought that a spreadsheet was boring and a five-year business plan was stupid. Now debits and credits are some of my most effective magical tools of transformation.

Today, the best business advice I could give is that it is most important to risk, stretch, persist, dream, get clear, and constantly refine your goals, objectives, and priorities. It is also critical for anyone starting a business to think outside of the box but still work within reality. Take baby steps at the beginning to test out your idea and your processes, but when the signs are right, don't be afraid to roll your project out.

Spiritually, I would advise any new businessperson to have faith in yourself and the business you are starting. Never forget that you are a part of God. Pray for guidance, meditate, visualize, and use affirmation and ritual wherever and whenever possible. Of course, there's no one true path to combining financial and spiritual success within a business. Some people will feel completely at home using visualization and ritual in their offices or homes; others will feel self-conscious or even silly. The most important thing is to adapt these principles and use them in the way that works best for you. To a greater or lesser extent, all successful businesses are the result of trial and error.

The trials and errors of *Magical Blend* are written here on these pages. I'm rarely pleased when I'm the person who makes those errors, but that comes with the territory. The other path, that of stasis and predictability, is not one that I would choose in my life or my business. For example, very recently we parted ways with several of our long-standing employees. They were wonderful people who understood our mission and loved the magazine. But they had grown stale here. They were no longer willing to adapt to fit our vision of where our magazines were headed. It was a painful decision, but one that was the right one for the business as well as the individuals involved.

Integrity and vision have been essential to *Magical Blend*'s continued existence. The issues of the magazine that come out today have little in common with the ones that came out in the early 1980s. I'm still involved and they still deal with spirituality and creativity. Yet the comics are gone. The poetry is gone. We seldom print fiction. The paper is different. The black and white line art has been replaced with color art and photos. We have moved the offices from San Francisco to Chico, in California's beautiful Northstate. There is a greater emphasis on health, travel, and music. The articles and interviews are much more concise and to the point. We have even rewritten our statement of purpose a number of times. Yet I feel the vision, intent, and integrity have remained constant. I have insisted that if we can't use the principles that we put into each issue in the office and in our dealings with printers, suppliers, writers, and artists, then they don't have any substance. That's not to say that there haven't been instances when we failed to live up to our own high standards. You could find people whose view of me or *Magical Blend* is somewhat less than glowing. Yet overall, we have attempted to bring a higher vision into all we do and how we do it. Most people who have worked for *Magical Blend* years later will tell you it was one of the best jobs that they ever had, as well as being a fantastic growth experience. I'm proud of that. In short, as long as it exists, *Magical Blend* will attempt to function as an enlightened business in every possible way.

Not everyone understands or even likes my commitment to this magazine. Even after more than 20 years together, my wife still wishes that I was a schoolteacher with a steady income and less risk at every turn of world events and the economy. My worldview has matured a great deal in 25 years. But that's natural. After all, I've spent nearly half my life as the publisher of *Magical Blend*. In those years, I've changed every bit as much as the magazine itself.

Yet, as I reread my journals from those early years, my basic beliefs have not changed. I believe that the humans alive on this planet today chose to be born at this time so that they can be involved in the end of history as we know it and the beginning of heaven on Earth. We have come to witness the last throes of a male-dominated, greed-oriented, selfish world. The Earth today is a school for potential gods and goddesses—that would be each of you reading these words. I further believe that each of us at each moment has the choice to decide how we want to think, perceive, react, or act upon everything in our immediate environment. Those decisions determine if we live in continuous, joyous ecstasy or miserable, perpetual pain and suffering. A truly deep and unwavering commitment to personal evolution as well as the evolution and improvement of humankind and nature will all but guarantee a life with greater amounts of joy and thankfulness.

For more than two decades, I have poured my heart into every issue of this magazine in order to make it more than a magazine. I go to sleep most nights believing that *Magical Blend* is making the world a better place. I am proud that every issue of *Magical Blend* and our new magazine, *Natural Beauty & Health*, is read by well over 120,000 people. I am excited that we are planning to launch two new magazines in the coming year, *Transitions*, for those 50 and over, and *Fresh Blend*, for those 30 and under.

This book will not establish me as an intellectual or an enlightened being far in advance of the rest of humanity. If anything, it will reveal me as an imperfect idealist who has had to make constant compromises to continue the growth of a magazine that he believed could and does make a difference in the world. Perhaps I am too proud of the fact that I had no business background. From the beginning until the present day, we have had little funding and no well-connected benefactors. Seldom has anyone on the staff had any experience with magazine publishing, or even the business world, before they came to us. Yet still we persisted and survived against some pretty awesome odds. *Magical Blend* still exists as a magazine that not only believes in the future, but has a role to play in helping to create it. If I am too proud of these things, I hope you will forgive me—my wife and friends sometimes do. But I am thankful for being a part of such a unique and wild expression of hope and vision. Why the gods and goddesses favored me in this way I might never know. But I don't plan on giving up until I die!

Some days I wonder, if I hadn't traveled to Mexico and Vera Cruz and later to San Francisco, what would my life have been? Would I have wandered aimlessly for all my existence searching for meaning and a mission? I'll never know; however, I give thanks daily for the wonderful work that I have been led to do. It has been one of the great blessings of my life.

I can promise you that the continued evolution of *Magical Blend* will be amazing, spiritual, emotional, hopeful, and, of course, magical. After all these years, I still see it as an amazing celebration of all the potentials found in life, Earth, humanity, and the future. I urge each of you reading this to please keep challenging yourself and the world around you, keep manifesting your dreams, keep challenging your understanding of reality, and keep working to open up your heart and your soul. Most of all, keep reading! The future of *Magical Blend*, like that of humanity, is a story that we write word by word, and day by day. Best of all, it's a tale that, from this point forward, we will all cocreate together.

Magical Blend magazine started in my living room in the Richmond district of San Francisco. It was an experiment to see if California's unique blend of edgy spirituality and creative outpourings could, in fact, change the world. This book is an attempt to "write down the bones" of that experiment—an experiment that we are still conducting, issue upon issue and year after year. These pages will tell you how *Magical Blend* came to be, what transpired during our evolution, who influenced our direction, and why we are the way we are. Along the way, I'll attempt to distill the lessons learned from a quarter century of running a spiritual business from the razor's edge. I have often used that term to refer to the balance between being a profitable business; publishing magazines that inspire, uplift, and make the world a better place; and running the organization both spiritually and efficiently while attempting to remain relatively sane. We seldom have all these elements balanced but that has always been the goal. For that reason and many others I believe that *Magical Blend*'s history is a tale worth telling, for it's a story filled with hope, love, ambition, setbacks, and triumph. It has indeed been one long, strange trip—and a magical one, at that.

I invite you to come along and relive the ride!

ONE

THE BEGINNING (1978–1979)

Magical Blend magazine's story could start in countless ways, places, and times. If everyone who was involved in the unfolding of *Magical Blend* told their version of the tale, there would be many very different versions. Many people played essential roles and contributed their blood, sweat, and tears. Each was important and I in no way wish to lessen any of their contributions. However I was one of the founders and have been the main publisher, editor, and leader for most of our 25 years. And I am writing this book. So that makes my story in some ways *Magical Blend*'s story.

I was born and raised in New England, about 30 miles north of Boston, in a small town called Methuen. I grew up on a farm surrounded by woods, across the street from a huge old cemetery. My father was a funeral director, as was his father before him. You could say that I grew up around death. This causes one to question things. Why are we born? What happens to us when we die?

Are there ghosts or spirits we can't see? Due to a childhood accident, I couldn't speak in a manner that anyone besides my family, close friends, and very patient and caring teachers could understand until I was nine years old. Thus words and their proper uses became very important to me from early on.

I attended college in Boston. During my junior year, I traveled to Peru and had several life-altering experiences. Eventually I returned to Boston and received my degree in political science. Then I couldn't decide if I desired to enter my father's business or not. While studying to get my embalmer's and funeral director's license in Nashville, Tennessee, I decided that I would rather have a life dedicated to improving the planet rather than burying the dead. I then tried my hand at many trades—teaching kindergarten, farming, working at a nuclear power plant, and fish mongering to name a few. But I was always drawn to writing and magazines. In Boston, I worked with a number of experimental publications, such as *The Open Door*, *The Parnassis Review*, *Poor Farm Comics and Stories*, and *Shot in the Dark*. They were all so experimental, weird, way out, and uncommercial that none lasted more than a few issues. I learned much of what not to do. Now, I grew up in the sixties and early seventies. The world was a wild place. Drugs and dreams of Utopian futures were the stuff of many lives. In New England, these beliefs all conspired to make me feel like an outsider. I didn't want to do things as they had always been done. I didn't just want my piece of the pie; I wanted to build new pie factories and feed the world joyously.

In the fall of 1977, I was attending a seminar in the Silva Mind improvement method. There was an exceptional instructor and it opened my life to a plethora of possibilities. It was at that seminar that I met Maria Nuez. We began dating and fell in love. We lived together the following spring and summer, all the while saving money so that we might hitchhike to Peru. I wanted badly to return and to share its other worldliness and its miracles with Maria.

In September, we drove a drive-away car to Boulder, Colorado. From there, we took a bus to Tucson, Arizona and then began hitching in Mexico. We had six weeks of fun and adventure from Tucson to Mexico City, from Acapulco to Oaxaca. Finally we arrived in Vera Cruz.

Vera Cruz, Mexico

We had been in Mexico for five weeks when Maria and I arrived in Vera Cruz, where we settled into a cheap hotel room on the edge of the tourist section of town. We washed up and laid our tired bodies down, but our hunger outweighed our exhaustion. So we got dressed, put all our cash and traveler's checks into our money belts (for the hotel room didn't seem secure) and headed downtown for dinner. We had been on a bus for two days so we indulged ourselves by going to a fancy restaurant. We ordered seafood Vera Cruz style and a big pitcher of sangria wine. The meal was divine. Afterwards we wandered around the tourist section window-shopping and listening to the oil drum bands. It all felt too "touristy," though, and after more than a month, we felt like hardened adventurers. The sangria might have been affecting our decision-making abilities, for even though the hour was late we went in search of nontourist sites and some adventure in the dark. Wow, did we ever find adventure.

We wandered into a bad section of town and proceeded down to the shorefront. Eventually we came to the entrance of a long, dark pier. We decided to see what the stars and sea looked like from the end. To get onto the pier we walked past a group of homeless hombres huddled around a fire. People in Mexico, except for the police in Oaxaca, had been so very nice to us that we didn't stop to question the situation we were entering as we passed these men on our way out to the end of a long, deserted pier. When we got to the end, we heard footsteps and turned around to discover the unthinkable.

The five men, one with a pipe and one with a knife, had followed us. When they saw us turn, they spoke harshly in Spanish and jumped us. I was immediately pummeled with fists and hit with the pipe. I fought back as best I could to protect us, but it was nearly useless. I felt the knife enter my side and the pipe smash down on my nose, knocking me unconscious. I passed out, with the knowledge that I had been stupid and that these men were raping the woman whom I loved and was traveling with. My last thought was, "Oh shit, they killed me. I'm dead!"

I awoke in a land of indescribable colors—bright hues and variances on our spectrum that I have never observed before or since. I wasn't even sure my physical body could perceive or my physical mind hold onto the subtly exquisite sights, sounds, and smells that I was experiencing. I stood up and felt my side and my nose. They were fine. As a matter of fact, I felt wonderful, perhaps better than I ever had. I attempted to orient myself.

I began to wonder. "This ain't right. I was just killed. My nose should be broken. My side should be hurt and bleeding. Where am I? Why do I feel so good? Am I dead? I didn't see any white light. This can't be real. I am dreaming in Mexico with Maria beside me, right? No, this isn't a dream. Shit, am I really dead?"

Then my very thought process shifted. Where was I? Where had I just been? Why did I feel this deep sense of fear and failure? Who had I let down? I was in a rural setting: rolling green hills with beautiful trees and, off in the distance, lakes and streams. Then, from the distance, I saw six people approaching me.

"OK," I thought. "If I'm dead, then these would be relatives, right? My grandparents? Nah! My old friends Gene Gravel or Mary Wooly? Nah! Those aren't relatives. Who are they? Angels? They look pretty weird for angels. None of this is out of any book I ever read. What about Maria? I hope she's alive and OK somewhere. These people are getting close and they're glowing!"

There were three women and three men, all of them appearing radiantly healthy and happy to see me. I could actually see their auras, which were mostly golden with violet and spring green rays shooting forth. I didn't have a clue who they were or where we were. They were dressed in what seemed like ceremonial garb of mostly green and gold. As they walked closer to me, they just smiled, yet it felt that they were radiating some form of warmth or healing energy right into the essence of my being. Their ethnic origin was unclear; their features seem to flow as I looked at them. One moment I was sure they were African, the next Asian, then Incan, then Native American, then European, then alien, and on and on. I found this disconcerting, so I spoke up. "Hi, who are you?" I asked. "Where am I? Is this a dream or am I dead?" At first, no one said anything, they just all looked at each other. Then a woman with an extremely purplish, golden aura stepped forward and said, "Please sit down." Her voice had an almost physical effect on me; it seemed like a warm massage. She proceeded, "It will take a while to make all that is happening clear to you. However, be at peace while you are here. You have all the time you can imagine. Let us talk to you about your life, the opportunities you have missed, the lessons you have learned, and the work you might yet choose to do."

I thought, "This has got to be a dream. It's more like a movie than anything I've ever lived through. They're going to tell me that I'm dead. Yeah, that's it—I have more time than I can imagine because I'm really dead. Oh shit, now what? I'll never get to see Peru or Boston again and the Inca Gods are really going to be pissed that I failed to keep our agreement. Now what? To die at 25—that just ain't right."

Then they each took turns talking. Actually, it was more like a telepathic music in my mind that I understood on many levels. I will never forget the experience and the general outline of the information that they gave me. They explained that all people are born with a number of possible alternative lives to be lived out. Each decision we make, they said, brings us into a different reality.

"OK," I answered. "If I'm getting this right, then I'm not really dead unless I agree to choose to be dead. Why would I ever do that? No, give me another chance! I promise that I won't blow it again! No more docks and no more stupid risks. Well not so many, anyway. Just give me my life back!"

They interrupted my thoughts by explaining firmly that due to my unique life and experiences up to this point, I was at a crucial crossroads. I could choose to die, go back to live as I had been, or step up my spiritual energies and accept a meaningful mission. They explained that the whole planet Earth was at a similar crossroads, that there were many powerful forces at work attempting to pull the planet in countless directions. The most difficult for them to accept were the forces attempting to keep the Earth's inhabitants in a zombielike state of victimization, generating energies of confusion, fear, and greed to be used for nefarious purposes. Those forces wanted to keep from us all the knowledge of each individual's limitless potential. They were conspiring to keep humanity in a state in which they could be controlled and shepherded as sheep.

These spiritual beings I was visiting with, on the other hand, represented a smaller force who were dedicated to setting free the god and goddess potential in each individual and every living thing on Earth. The planet Earth was originally intended and designed to be a school for gods and goddesses. They were dedicated to assisting people in waking up and taking full advantage of the fact that humanity has free will. They felt strongly that spiritual energies were as important as scientific principles or material existence or even group ceremonies. Following any leaders was deadly by their standards, for to follow leaders is to give away your own power. It is better to decide what is best for yourself, for each individual has within all the answers they need about what is right for them. This is a thumbnail version of the things that were explained to me.

When the beings had gone into enough of the details to allow me to understand their views, they offered me an opportunity to play a catalyst role in sharing this information in forms that could make a major difference in the planet Earth's future. It wouldn't be easy, they said, and they could offer me very few guideposts along the way. They assured me that this work would complement that of the Incan gods and goddesses I had agreed to take on years before. They could set me on the path if I wanted them to, but I would have to find my guidance, as I would help others to do, from within. I would be working for the underdogs and the odds would be against my success. Then, if I succeeded, I would have to be careful not to become confused. I was only to act as a catalyst, one who provided liberating information to those ready to hear it. I should not ever let my ego or personality take over or think the fame that might come was more important than setting others free. I was never to set myself off as better than others.

This was only some of what we talked about. We sat and talked for what seemed like days. I do remember in the course of our conversation coming to love these beings and their goals. I wanted nothing more than to dedicate my life to sharing a role in their mission. I don't remember them spelling out any of the details of how I was to play out this role of catalyst. Yet that didn't seem to bother me at the time.

I remember thinking something like, "OK, I can live as I had been living. That almost got me killed. Or I can team up with these amazing cosmic beings working to help humanity and the planet Earth. This is like a comic book! Are you kidding? Where do I sign up?"

Eventually they all stood up and stared at me. "Then it is agreed—your time is not up. You must go back. You have very important work that you have agreed to dedicate your life to. This is your choice. You are extremely clear that you can refuse it and make other choices. We only offer it to help set up the opportunities. You must make the commitment. Even if you commit now, it is only for now; you will have to recommit on a regular basis." I fell all over myself assuring them I had made my decision.

Then one of them waved her hand and what seemed like a shimmering pool appeared. I looked in and I saw myself crumpled on the pier in Vera Cruz in a pool of blood. The desperadoes were holding Maria down and raping her. At first I felt oddly detached. I felt pity for the men and Maria—even for myself—because they weren't in this spiritual dimension and could not imagine its wonderfulness. The pool continued to attract my attention, but the way in which it did so began to change. I became more involved, more concerned; I became sickened and angry to the core of my being. The glorious feelings I had been sharing with these spiritual beings began slipping away. I experienced a sense of vertigo, disorientation, and great pain. I seemed to fall into the shimmering picture.

The next thing I knew, I was back on the pier. I was angry, scared, excited, thankful, confused—you name it. I had every possible emotion racing through me. Without thinking, I leaped to my feet and began screaming like a banshee. I couldn't believe those noises were coming out of my mouth. They sounded unearthly and full of believable death threats. Wherever the noises came from, they were effective. The five men jumped off Maria, grabbed our money and her pants, and ran like hell. I continued screaming until I could no longer see them. Then I limped over to Maria and attempted to soothe her. "They raped me again and again, all of them. I thought you were dead. They thought you were dead. If you weren't dead, why did you lay there so still while they did this to me?" Then she cried and cried in my arms. I gave her my pants and she ripped my shirt to bandage my side. She had no major physical injuries beyond bruises and soreness but her damages were deeper than mine. We limped all the way back to our hotel half naked and bleeding. Once we got there we explained to the hotel clerk what had happened. We were both in shock. We were very confused. Maria hadn't lost consciousness and was extremely traumatized. I attempted to be as supportive as I could but I could feel her deep dark hole of terror and violation. My stories of other-dimensional visions were not met with a receptive audience and understandably so.

Our hotel manager spoke broken English and we, poor Spanish. Luckily, we had paid for our room when checking in. After we got washed up and changed, he called the police, the hospital, and a cab. We went to the hospital, where they bandaged me up and examined Maria and gave us some medicine to calm us down and lessen the pain. Then we went to the police and made a report. Just before sunrise, we returned to our hotel room and collapsed. We slept for 36 hours. When we did emerge, the helpful hotel clerk showed us the write-up in the newspaper and sent us to the American Express office. Due to the tremendous exchange rate on the streets, we had been carrying most of our savings in cash. That was gone. However, we were given new travelers checks to replace those that were taken. The American embassy issued us temporary passport papers.

Finding ourselves with little money, and now fearful of everything in Mexico, we decided to take the train back to the border. Maria had been offered a good job in San Francisco before we left our Boston home, so that seemed like a good place to go and regroup for the winter.

The rape was forever a sickness or boil below the surface between Maria and me. On the surface she forgave me. Yet I had failed her at a crucial moment of need and neither of us could truly forgive me for that. Beyond that, while she suffered this terrible abuse and personal violation, all the time thinking that I was dead, I had been off visiting with beautiful cosmic beings, being given spiritual wisdom and a superhero's assignment. It never really mattered on some level that I returned and saved her. It was the failure, desertion, and violation that sat like a sick hippopotamus between us from that night forward. Maria was very brave, spiritual, strong, and forgiving, but she also lived in denial, never wanting to talk about her unresolved issues, never going to therapy, and never able to fully heal or forgive me. I was naively happy to join her in her denial and did not care to discuss the events of that night beyond my visions. I wish I had been wiser, a better healer, and more aware. I believe life unfolds as it is meant to; however, if I had those following years to live over again, I would take more meaningful actions to help Maria heal. As it was, I was young and rather insensitive. I had to learn slowly.

San Francisco, California

After walking across the border in Nogales, we hitchhiked to the Bay Area. It took us another week, but we felt much safer back in the U.S. of A. As fate would have it, we arrived in San Francisco on Halloween 1978. We found a room in a youth hostel in the Tenderloin District and went to the Castro for San Francisco's very own version of the Mardi Gras. It was on that night that it started to dawn on me just how different San Francisco was from Boston.

Maria and I began exploring the city. It didn't take me very long to fall in love with San Francisco. I felt then that Northern California in general and San Francisco in particular offered an open-minded acceptance that is quite rare in the world. On the East Coast, I had always felt that the prevailing attitude was, "Don't do something different; it won't be worth the effort." On the West Coast, however, the attitude felt more like, "Please do something different; we will help you and the world will be better for it." San Francisco offered fertile ground in which the ideas implanted in me at Vera Cruz might bloom.

I was amazed at the plethora of classes and seminars in the San Francisco area. I took classes on everything from creative visualization to astral traveling. I was exposed to ideas and spiritual ways of being that in previous years I could not have conceived of. It was as if my learning quotient had been greatly accelerated.

Maria started working almost immediately at the job that had been promised her, but it took me about a week to find employment. My first job in the Bay Area was as a childcare counselor in a group home in the suburb of Fremont. The clients were emotionally disturbed children between the ages of six and eleven. I worked and lived in the home each week from Wednesday at noon to Saturday at 5 P.M. The kids responded quite well to lovingly set limits and lots of exhausting attention. The job paid just above minimum wage, but all my meals were free and it gave me the chance to do a great deal of thinking about my future.

That fall and winter were full of adjustments to the West Coast. But that whole time while adjusting to California, what kept coming back to me were the other-dimensional words, "You have important work to do." I recall one class in particular that we took on astral travel, which was taught by a man from India. Both Maria and I discovered that we could do it with a good amount of focused intent. We also signed up for a weekly class on chakras, lead by two wonderful teachers and psychics, Bill Farr and Susan Sun. I paid Bill for a personal psychic reading. He said that Maria and I weren't going to be life mates. Furthermore, he predicted that I would meet a very strong willed, dark haired women from New England, that she and I had lots of important work to do together, and we would get married. ("No way! Never!" I remember thinking.) He also said that in the near future, I would be the leader of a very important organization that would be doing very unique and very important spiritual work. He was a great guy and very enthusiastic and positive, but I remember thinking that I might have wasted my money. I didn't see the likelihood of any of these things happening.

The Most Talented People in the World

Maria and I stayed at our youth hostel residence center until the end of November. Of course, the fact that we didn't have much money factored into our decision to stay there longer than we had originally planned, but there was more to it than that. What made it especially tough to leave were all the great people we had met there. Take Michael Epstein, for example. One afternoon, I noticed him in the kitchen, eating his soup and salad without utensils. I remember thinking that this man is either stark raving mad, an amazing attention-getter, or just has no regard for the norms of society. I wanted to get to know him better and figure him out. Well, I'm not sure that I ever fully figured out Michael. Like me, he grew up in the Northeast—Connecticut, in his case. He had been living in India before we met. He knew a great deal about every religion, cult, and New Age belief. Much of his adult life had been spent traveling around the world, and he spoke seven languages. Michael Epstein was a fairly eccentric man who greatly assisted in launching *Magical Blend*.

Then there was Jeff Fletcher, a brilliant student at the Art Institute. He worked part time in the hostel's dining room, even though his father owned the Fletcher organ empire down in Florida. Needless to say, he was a millionaire (the old man, not Jeff). Jeff knew things about art and artists that I had never imagined. He took Maria and I to a show of visionary artists in the greater San Francisco area. I had never seen such art before—so natural and other dimensional at the same time. I loved it. Attending that show with Jeff truly opened me up to the fact that many spiritual truths that words could only hint at were communicated in a better, clearer way through art. Jeff understood some of the basic elements of business from his father's example, and he had a knack for explaining art and writing in ways I never thought of before. Another eccentric!

I also recall meeting a charming, good-looking guy by the name of Tony who was a bit of a Casanova. Much to my relief, Maria was a bit irritated by him. Tony took us to a Sunday mass at Glide Memorial, a Methodist church with a charismatic, unorthodox minister, the Reverend Ceil Williams. He saw religion as an expression of creativity and charity, and his services were celebrations of life. This approach to spirituality as a way to celebrate life was a wonderful thing to see. Glide helped me begin to realize that spirituality was only truly valid if you lived it every moment of your life, and only meaningful if you could use it to help make the world a better place.

In some ways, Tony's counterpoint in the hostel was Carmen Lorata. She was beautiful, charming, brilliant, and was always dating a different man—but never for very long. She had grown up in Costa Rica and was a graduate student of journalism at the University of California at Berkley. Maria and she hit it off tremendously, and although Carmen and I flirted quite a bit, Maria was unthreatened by it.

The three of us would often attend poetry readings, book signings, and classes in writing as a spiritual tool. We would write together and critique each other's styles. Carmen taught Maria and me much about classical and professional writing, and she also introduced us to many new and upcoming authors. Carmen loved our writing, yet felt that her own was hampered by too much formality. She found Maria's work to be very technical yet from the heart, while mine broke most of the rules but was wild and sometimes fascinating. Back then I never suspected that Carmen would play an important role in my own evolution as well as the magazine's for the next five years.

We had the pleasure of meeting another important character at that time. Bill Tucker lived and worked at the hostel. He was a hardworking, rather funny, quite personable, likeable, smart, and short man. He was another person who would play a big role in my life later on, but I didn't imagine it back then.

One of my fellow counselors at the group home was a guy by the name of Val Baldwin. At the time, Val was a graduate student at San Jose State and very much into creative visualization. He was the first person to get me to fully understand the power and potential every person has if they focus their will and intent on their goals by using effective creative visualization. We became friends immediately.

For an article in our first issue, Val wrote, "Visualization is the art of creating your environment through the conscious use of your imagination. . . . All parts of the Universe being connected, by visualizing we bring our thoughts (images) into our physical surroundings due to the law of magnetic attraction. We influence our futures directly with our thought."

Soon after Val and I became friends he would drive up to San Francisco and Maria, Val, and I, along with whoever else was around and interested, would dedicate an hour to visualizing a wonderfully successful magazine that would have a positive effect on many people. I believed those sessions greatly helped in the coming launch of *Magical Blend.*

I also worked overlapping shifts on Saturdays for two hours with another great colleague, Joe Blondo. He had a master's degree in psychology and was a poetry fanatic. He lived for poetry, and he wrote some of the greatest verse I had ever read. He was able to express, or at least hint poetically, at many spiritual concepts that I couldn't clearly pin down in my writing. Joe spent countless hours sharing with me his spiritual poetry from countless other times and cultures. As fine as I knew Joe's poetry was, he had been rejected from every poetry journal that he ever submitted his work to.

In our first issue we printed a short poem from Joe. It read, in part:

Drifting through Time
Only part of me
Has been going
I walk out the door
Half there I communicate with myself
By long distance
As I walk I'm a jigsaw puzzle
Leaving a trail of pieces
Should I wonder
Why people have difficulty
Picking up
On me.

This simple, fun poem says much more than it appears to on the first read. So did Joe.

These people that I have mentioned are only a small number of a very large and colorful group of characters that Maria and I met in those early days. Throughout this time, we kept having serendipitous meetings with extremely talented artists, poets, writers, and spiritual teachers around San Francisco. It was wonderful to meet and get to know so many amazing individuals, all living in one small city at one tiny moment in time. They were very creative in original ways, all trying to express important spiritual notions that most people never heard of before. These were, I felt and still believe, some of the most talented people in the world. Many of them felt frustrated that there were so few avenues to share their insights and unique creative works with the world.

By the end of November, we finally moved out of the hostel in favor of a small, rather rough but furnished apartment nearby. We had had enough of communal dining and living by then. It was great to come and go as we pleased, and to visit only with those we wanted when we wished. Maria and I began writing down some of the ideas that were popping up in our heads all the time. Many of these thoughts developed into full-blown articles and stories, some of which we began submitting to magazines. Just as quickly, we began receiving rejection slips. Most said in one way or another that what we had submitted was well written but not appropriate for their magazine. The problem was that there really weren't any magazines at that time publishing the kind of things we wanted to say. Without being fully conscious of it, the essence of the thing that would eventually be *Magical Blend* was beginning to coalesce in our minds.

Discovering a Mission

Early in 1979, we moved out of our dingy little apartment and into a sweet beach cottage on a hill with 57 steps leading up to it. It was great to leave the dense Tenderloin district for the open, fresh air of San Francisco's Sunset neighborhood.

One day that spring, my sister Elizabeth showed up on the

doorstep of our new house and asked to move in with us. She needed to spend time away from New England. Of course she was lovely, but she wanted to do everything with us. We strongly encouraged her to get a job and told her she should save money to rent her own apartment. In many exciting ways Elizabeth's presence gave us renewed ambition and inspiration. Maria and I were tired of rejection slips and were openly talking about a creative project that could get our writing (along with the writing and art of all of our other talented new friends) out into the world. But did we dare start our own magazine? It seemed a huge leap, but one that we were increasingly committed to taking.

Soon after coming to live with us, Elizabeth began dating Bill Tucker, and before you knew it, they had moved in together. Maria and I missed Elizabeth's energy around the house, but by now we were both well on our way toward birthing our magazine project. In most ways, Elizabeth can be credited in being the catalyst for *Magical Blend,* for her presence pushed Maria and I to get off our duffs and begin cocreating our project. She and Bill stayed in our social circle and helped out greatly in birthing *Magical Blend* for the next couple of years, and then they moved to San Diego for work and the weather. Throughout this time, it seemed as though all we talked about was the magazine. Maria switched jobs and began to work for an astrology software company. She worked up an astrology conception chart on our magazine idea and it seemed that it would be very successful. We had decided that we would take the money we had saved to that point and use it to put out an issue of our new venture rather than buy a car or take a trip to Europe as we had planned. Our working titles were either *No Promises* or *Creativity and Spirituality Can Sell.*

Looking back on it now, it all seems so inevitable. From our terrible experience in Mexico to the decision to plunge ourselves into our publishing enterprise, less than eight months had passed. Yet we had both changed in many ways in that short period of time. The words of the beings who had visited me that night on the pier kept coming back to me again and again: "You have very important work that you must dedicate your life to." This magazine idea felt like the right path to begin fulfilling that mission. As the next step in the process, we began to gather material for the magazine. We decided to undertake an extensive letter-writing campaign to all the famous people who we respected and admired, and whose addresses were available. We explained that we were starting a magazine to be dedicated to the exploration of spirituality and the expansion of creativity. We asked them to write something that we could use in our first issue.

Around that time (the beginning of June), I received a phone call from an old acquaintance from back East, Angela Stella. She informed me that my old friend Verge Belanger was living with his wife, Jackie, and their new son, Benjamin, across the bay in Oakland. Verge is a character worth noting like few others. Verge and I went to Northern Essex Community College in Haverhill, Massachusetts in the early 1970s. Angela had given me Verge's address, so Maria and I took a trip over the Bay Bridge to visit. Verge and Jackie were excited to see us. They both were working day jobs but were very interested in a creative outlet as well. They thought that a magazine would be lots of fun. Verge and I had run the Northern Essex literary magazine for two years. He always loved the underground newspaper I produced in high school and even helped out a bit on *Poor Farm Comics and Stories* and *The Shot in the Dark* magazines I had published in New England after college. We began to have regular planning meetings about our new project; however, from very early on it was clear that we had different views of what this magazine was to be about. Verge and Jackie were emphatic that everything we published should have basis in science, not spirituality. Naturally, Maria and I strongly disagreed. Verge and Jackie resigned from the project almost before it had even begun, much to their and my great disappointment. However, a few months later, they reconsidered and were essential in helping us create and distribute the first year's worth of issues.

Meanwhile, Maria and I moved again, sadly giving up our lovely but rather expensive sublet at the beach in favor of a more reasonable shared house on Ashbury Street. This house stood just two blocks up from the Haight, right across the street from where the Jefferson Airplane were formed and lived at their sixties peak. The place definitely resonated with a great deal of magic. Our four English housemates were all into Alistair Crowley, the famous author of occult literature from the turn of the century. He was also one of the founding members of the famous metaphysical society called the Golden Dawn. His magic was a bit dark for my taste but fascinating nevertheless.

We continued have serendipitous meetings (or remeetings) with creative and interesting people. Maria and I were shopping at the Rainbow health food store and who should be our checker but my old astrologer and artist friend Renaldo from the Turtle Café in Cambridge. We invited him to dinner and I explained our project to him. He got excited and offered his help. Renaldo had all kinds of great contacts in the city, for he had been living for two years in San Francisco's gay and tremendously creative Castro District. He introduced us to William Stewart, who grew up on Cape Cod and went to Reed College with an old girlfriend of mine. William was a professional calligrapher and designer who also offered his help with our still-untitled magazine.

One day on the bus, Maria was creating an astrology chart when she met a man who was doing the same. His name was Jerry Snider, a very handsome and charming southern gentleman about our age. He was from Missouri by way of New Orleans. He was doing his charts for characters in a novel he was writing. In addition to his writing, Jerry did typesetting and editing for a small insurance magazine and he knew lots about layout to boot. Maria told him about our magazine idea and he came by a few days later to discuss it. I told him about Renaldo and William, mentioning that they were extremely talented but also very gay. Then I realized that Jerry was gay as well. I apologized.

So what! Whether gay, black, Latino, Asian, Native American, Moslem, dwarf, or loud French-Irish reformed Catholic from New England, in this project we were all to be equals. I love diversity, and all those different perspectives would certainly add flavor and depth to the magazine. It was clear that Jerry would be a great asset; I hoped that I hadn't offended him with my insensitive and narrow-minded way of talking about William and Renaldo.

Maria and I had been arguing for weeks about the name for the magazine. Since we were having such a difficult time agreeing, we decided to make a game of it. Both of us agreed that the title should be two words, so we each wrote down ten options. Neither of us liked any of the combinations selected by the other, so we ripped them all in half, put the individual words in a bowl and picked two out. The words we selected were "Magical" and "Blend." It was agreed! Our magazine would hereafter be known as *Magical Blend*. We would blend unrelated subjects as creatively and magically as Walt Disney once did. We chose the subtitle, *The Magazine of Synergy*. The term "synergy" was one of Buckminster Fuller's favorites. It essentially means that the whole of a thing is greater than the sum of its parts.

Most of the famous people whom we wrote to never responded. One who did was an author whose work I admired— John Nelson. He had written a transformative novel that I loved that was entitled *Starborn*. This was a great story about reincarnation and soul groups, all told from a child's perspective. He wrote back to say that he was in Hollywood making his book into a movie and was too busy to write anything for us. He wished us good luck anyway, which was very nice. We received only a few letters like that. John was another person who would be very important to myself and *Magical Blend* later on, but receiving his letter at that time was certainly a disappointment.

We also received a letter back from one of my all-time favorite science fiction and fantasy authors, Michael Moorcock. He had written the Eternal Champion series and the Elric Sword and

Sorcery series. He sent us an article from England that hadn't yet been published in the United States. He said that we could use it and his name free of charge if we wished. Dane Rudyar, the best and most original New Age astrologer of the time, also replied, saying that we could reprint any part of any of his books, also for free. In the piece we chose to print in issue #1, Dane stated: "Man is indeed a question of 'resonance' and the future science will come to learn that power can and should be released by resonating to various modalities of cosmic power, rather than by destroying them." These words are still important today!

Justin Green, a very wellknown underground artist and writer, thought by many to be almost as important as R. Crumb, sent us copies of some comics he did that were appropriate and said we could use them. Free once again! The title of it was *Visualization and Concentration*. In it, he stated, "Just like a windmill harnesses wind into mechanical energy, your visualization faculties convert dim motives into concrete images. . . . When you concentrate on these . . . your unconscious will deliver you a bonus package. You can and will manifest what you focus on. . . . Life will unlock its most precious secrets to those folks who can concentrate and visualize at will."

We also received cartoons by a then little-known cartoonist named William Van Horn. His one-page comic received great response and his work appeared in every one of our next ten issues. He went on to become a best-selling children's book writer and illustrator in Australia and the head comics artist for Disney's European comics.

So Michael Moorcock, Dane Rudyar, Justin Green, and William Van Horn were the only ones who responded positively to the countless letters that we had sent out. However, we felt hopeful that their names would help get people's attention, make the proper statement about what our themes and emphasis were, and sell lots of magazines.

By September, things were really rolling. People kept coming into our path that would have a great impact on the magazine. For example, Maria began taking classes from a woman by the name of Jomaro—a highly developed spiritual person, psychic, and writer. Maria also met this amazing whale and nature muralist in Berkeley, Dan Gold. I felt that he was very attracted to Maria; however, he was a nice guy and very talented, with so many artist and writer contacts that I ignored my jealousy as much as possible. Dan introduced us to a number of amazingly creative folks. One of the most interesting was John Oberdorf, an arch conservative, Republican, pipe/cigar smoking, scotch drinking, amateur anthropologist. He was a military officer's son who had lived on army bases all over the world. Another wonderful artist Dan introduced us to was Eddie Willie, a Native American law student with some strong politics and lovely artwork. In one of Eddie's comics that we printed in the first issue, he has Morning Cloud, a Native American shaman, performing an Earth renewal ceremony where she calls on the great spirit to protect our land and to keep it pure and free from desecration. This plea is even more relevant today than it was 25 years ago.

When Verge and Jackie Belanger agreed to return to the project that fall, all of the pieces were in place. They even brought along their friend Antro Allie, who taught tarot and psychic classes, in addition to creating terrific plays. He was a wonderful writer who agreed to write for us.

The mission, the people, and the city all combined to give Maria and I the sense that we were ready to unveil a new way of thinking to the world. All that we were sure of was that *Magical Blend* would be unlike anything anyone had ever seen before. Most of us involved in the project were in our twenties, filled with optimism and hope that we could indeed change the planet if only we could reach enough readers. Looking back now, it's funny how little has changed. I'm still full of hope and optimism, and I still believe that with each new reader, we're helping change the world just a little bit. Of course, back then we were still scratching our heads about how we would do all of the editing, layout, printing, distributing, etc. But all of that reality was still in our future. Just then we were all living in the worlds of dreams and unlimited potential.

T W O

THE BIRTH OF *MAGICAL BLEND*—
ISSUES 1–4 (1980–1981)

How Do We Do This, Exactly?

The first issue of *Magical Blend*, symbolically, took nine months to be born. Maria and I had first discussed the concept of the magazine in May of 1979, and the first issue appeared in February of 1980. None of us involved had business training, and there were a multitude of lessons ahead of us about producing a spiritually creative magazine in a materialistic, dog-eat-dog business climate. We learned our lessons slowly. We had no financial backing and seldom had enough money to print an issue. For our first few years, *Magical Blend* was a labor of love with an amazingly dedicated volunteer staff. We worked on the magazine nights and weekends, working day jobs to support ourselves. We donated any money left over after rent and food to printing the magazine. Those were challenging times when we were not sure if *Magical Blend* could survive, never mind become an international force. However, each of our early issues embodied the following statement of purpose:

> *Magical Blend* accepts the premise that society is undergoing a fundamental transformation. A new worldview is being born, and whether this birth is to be an easy or difficult one depends largely upon the individual. It is our aim to chart the course this transformation is taking and assist the individual to cope with and contribute to the birthing process. We believe that people's thoughts influence their reality; if this is true then the world we live in is a combination of our highest hopes, our deepest fears, and the whole range of experiences that fall between. Our goal is to embrace the hopes, transform the fears, and discover the magical behind the mundane. In this way, we hope to act as a catalyst to encourage the individual to achieve his or her highest level of spiritual awareness. We endorse no one pathway to spiritual growth but attempt to explore many alternative possibilities to help transform the planet.

This statement of purpose sums up what I have dedicated my life to. Using this as our guiding light, and learning about business as we went, we got through those first years, printing issues when we could and distributing them however possible.

The events surrounding the writing, design, and layout of that first issue are still fresh in my memory even after all these years. The apartment that Maria and I had rented on Ashbury Street became ground zero of the *Magical Blend* experience, with all of our new and old friends dropping by, often at strange hours, to contribute to the magazine. The feeling of teamwork and camaraderie was wonderful and at times intense, for we all were all equally passionate about the *Magical Blend* mission.

During the last few weeks of 1979, events picked up a momentum of their own. The pressure really came on during one weekend early in December, just before the issue was due to be sent to the printer. We were at the Ashbury street apartment, which overflowed with all sorts of characters. Some were pasting up typeset pages and even simply typed-up versions of poems, articles, stories, and line drawings. Tons of people were there around the clock working and reworking page layouts and proofreading as much as possible. We had to lock Michael Epstein in a room and give him cocaine every half hour (this was the 1970s, after all) in order for him to finish a great story that he had begun. When he would slide another 200 new words of the story out under the door we would slide the drugs back under to him. The story turned out great. In it Michael has the U.S. president broker an amnesty between God and Lucifer. My favorite lines were, "God accused Lucifer of corrupting his children to knowledge without truth. Lucifer answered that God was on a heavy moralistic trip and that the most important thing was that their children be free to find their own truth." Now, God and Lucifer agreeing to find common ground and compromising for the good of humanity still sounds enlightened to me.

We were under a tight deadline because the San Francisco printer that we found had told us that his broken presses would be fixed by Tuesday morning, and that we would be his first job if we had the deposit and the issue all ready to go. About 2 A.M. on Monday morning, Verge realized that we had spelled his name wrong on the masthead. I was so tired and frustrated that I screamed at him, "Verge, we can't get everything just perfect!" Of course, I immediately felt terrible, yelling at him after he had worked so hard, so long, and so well.

Actually, everyone who was there that long weekend went way beyond the call of duty. Jeff Fletcher and his German girlfriend, along with another female friend from Nepal, helped tremendously with layouts. Renaldo, Jerry, and William did an unbelievable amount of highly professional graphic design work. Carmen

Lorata did massive amounts of copyediting and proofing, while Elizabeth and Bill were there doing whatever they could to keep everyone's spirits up and make it work. Jomaro, Joe Blondo, Val Baldwin, Dan Gold, John Oberdorf, and Eddie Willie all came by and assisted in various ways.

Early on Tuesday morning, Maria, Renaldo, William, Jerry, Carmen, and I were just about ready to bring the issue to the printer when an argument broke out. Renaldo had, at the last minute, drawn a well-rendered but ridiculous monkey picture, and he insisted that we use it as the illustration for the final article, from the famous astrologer, Dane Rudyar. We refused to use the monkey art, feeling that it gave the wrong message. Renaldo got furious and said that we either use it or we couldn't use any of his art in the issue (which included the logo design and the cover). Maria refused to budge; so did Renaldo. The argument became all-inclusive, fired and fueled by all the intensity, frustration, exhaustion, compromises, and disappointments caused by the first issue not being exactly what any one of us separately had envisioned.

Maria and Renaldo had had it with each other. They had never really clicked and had been pulling the initial issue in two very different directions for many months. Both of them had worked very hard and made some of the most extreme compromises in their separate versions of what the issue should consist of and look like. At this point their frustration and anger began being vented on me. They were fed up with me making all the major decisions, especially since I rarely consulted anyone who didn't happen to be in the room with me at the time. Their perception was that I was taking all the credit for other people's ideas and hard work and they were tired of it.

The argument went on and on, and the attacks and counterattacks grew mean and then vicious. William, Jerry, and Carmen all sided with me and told Maria and Renaldo to stop their attacks. They said that I had been the one to bring both of their wonderful, inspired, and diverse visions together, and that I had been most important in coordinating the melding together of opposing viewpoints into something better than either of them or any of us could do on our own. We had all cocreated a great first issue from the compromises that were made, so they begged one last time for us to leave out the damn monkey art, keep the rest of the magazine the way it was, and bring it immediately to the printer.

That was way too much for Renaldo and Maria! They both felt undermined and their roles lessened. Renaldo shouted, "No! No more compromises on this terrible and silly project!" He scooped up all of his work and left, never to be published in our pages. Maria then announced that she was withdrawing her writing and wanted her name stricken from the masthead. It was obvious, she said, that the magazine had become more important to me than her or our relationship. So, not only was she resigning from *Magical Blend,* she was in no uncertain terms breaking up with me! She promptly gathered her things and moved in with a friend.

The rest of us were exhausted, stunned, and crushed. Without Maria's writing or Renaldo's logo, cover, and illustrative work (both of which dominated the issue) what would we do? Without Maria how could I continue to exist? I had let the creation of *Magical Blend,* my ego, my need to lead, and my overcompensation for a fear of failure and a multitude of self doubts destroy the best relationship I had ever experienced to that point in my life. I was devastated and immobilized.

Now, years later, I have come to understand some important lessons about that intense period of time. Maria and I were together for more than two years, during which we were sharing a major responsibility, not only in attempting to create and set a tone for *Magical Blend* but also in trying to find time for our "real" jobs and each other. I don't think either of us ever recovered from Vera Cruz; it was mainly the tremendous cooperative effort that we poured into *Magical Blend* which had kept us together.

I think that after the first issue actually was all laid out and ready for the printer, Maria was exhausted and scared. She could see *Magical Blend* eventually turning into something big and real, and that wasn't what she had ever wanted. Plus my intensity and other shortcomings have a tendency to wear people down over a prolonged period of time.

Without the work done by Renaldo and Maria, if we were ever going to truly bring *Magical Blend* magazine into existence, we needed to choose other good writings that we had held out for possible use in future issues and redesign almost three-quarters of the magazine. The thought of doing this was daunting. William, Jerry, and Carmen leaped heroically into the void.

By that Thursday, we had finished rebuilding and reworking the issue. It was a very different magazine without Maria's writing or Renaldo's artwork, but different in many great ways. The logo William designed was rather Disneyland-like and much more professional, inviting, and attractive than what Renaldo had come up with. We used the logo that William created in two days for the next 18 years because it said to us that the magic we were addressing was similar to that of Walt Disney—fun, uplifting, entertaining, life enhancing, and helpful.

We chose an inspired line drawing by John Oberdorf for the cover art. William made all the layouts appear much smoother and less amateurish. Most of them seemed less like cartoons and more like the artwork that one would find from the finest New York publishers. The reworking greatly improved our first issue.

William, Jerry, Carmen, and I delivered what was destined to be the first issue of *Magical Blend* to the printer that afternoon. On the masthead, Carmen had replaced Maria as my co-publisher/editor because she had done so much and was essential to the creation, decision-making, and details that went into the issue. William and Jerry were listed next as design and production. In fact, they had done much more than just that, so we listed them both twice. Jerry appeared again with Verge as typography, and William showed up again for cover and logo design.

We were all very proud of what we felt was a much-improved

version of the magazine we almost printed. However, due to our delay, our printer said that he had to start another big job first. He told us that it would now take three or four weeks to get the magazine printed, but at that point, we were in no mood to argue. We dropped the magazine off, went home, and slept well for the first time in days.

New Year 1980 came and went, and still our printer hadn't done anything on our magazine. He said that his negative camera and plate machines were broken and it looked like it might be another month before he could even get started. By this time, Carmen had gotten me a new job at Carlos Goldstein's, a restaurant/bar where she worked during the day. I became the 6 P.M. through closing time bartender and evening manager.

By a wonderful stroke of luck, our boss Tom Counter, a very charismatic bar manager who often performed magic tricks for the customers, knew of a printer in Sacramento. Tom called this printer on our behalf and reported that the printer was willing to do us a favor and print our magazine fast and inexpensively. So, we decided to pull the job back from the excuse-making guy in San Francisco in favor of Tom's friend at Spellman Printing in Sacramento.

Early in February, Tom and I drove back down to Sacramento and picked up the first few copies of the first issue "hot off the presses," as they say. It certainly wasn't perfect but that first issue was something unique and wonderful, overflowing with promise, hope, and magic. I'm still so very proud of it.

The next week, I was home alone when a truck pulled up and delivered 20,000 copies of the magazine. I called everyone I could think of to help me haul the load inside, but they were all at work. So I carried all 400 boxes up two flights of stairs and down the long hallway by myself—one box at a time. It's a good thing that I was young and strong! We were left with no room in the apartment except some narrow pathways to the bed, toilet, and sink, but the magazines were there, in our possession. What an incredible feeling of accomplishment.

Within a few days, everyone we knew in San Francisco dropped by to get a copy of *Magical Blend*. They were all impressed at how well it was written, designed, and printed. It looked like we had a winner on our hands.

Communal Living

Soon after our first issue came out, it became obvious that Carmen and I worked extremely well together as copublishers and were becoming very good friends. We had different work schedules at Carlos Goldstein's, as she worked from 10 A.M. to 6 P.M., and I from 6 P.M. until 2 or even 3 A.M.

She hated her present roommates and I wanted to leave the apartment Maria and I had once shared. We agreed that because we had such different schedules and were such good friends, we would probably make great roommates, so we began looking for a big apartment that we could share and use as *Magical Blend*'s meeting and working center. We fairly quickly found and rented an inexpensive, spacious, four-bedroom apartment, with a huge living room and large kitchen, on the top floor of a three-story apartment building on the corner of 20th and Florida Streets in the Mission District. It was a location that was destined to go down in the history of *Magical Blend*.

It turned out that the offices of Last Gasp Underground Comics were just down the street. We introduced ourselves to Ron Turner, the founder and owner of Last Gasp, and showed him our first issue. Ron was friendly with every major underground artist in the world, and he told us about The Cosmic Brain Trust, an Oakland-based group who were printing spiritual comics and the like. Ron thought that we and this Cosmic Brain Trust outfit had a lot in common and perhaps we might work together, so he gave us their address and phone number. We wasted no time in contacting them and arranging a meeting.

The next day, Carmen and I took the bus to Oakland and hiked to the section where the Brain Trust was located. We arrived and found ourselves awed to meet Ray Sun, Miron Murcury, Melissa Snow Wind, and Mark Roland. What an amazing group of creative and spiritual artists! Our arrival was auspicious, for The Cosmic Brain Trust had just agreed to break up.

In their shared time as a group they had created and published a number of comic books and small-run experimental magazines. Carmen and I loved some of what they had published. Distributing and selling their creative out pouring had been an insurmountable challenge for them. This had caused all of them varying degrees of disappointment and disillusionment. The lease on their house had just expired and Ray, their leader, had decided to move to Los Angeles to try his hand in a larger entertainment arena. Miron had found a room for himself a few blocks away, but the lovely couple, Melissa and Mark, were about to be homeless.

We all hit it off wonderfully. They were so excited and impressed with the first issue of *Magical Blend* that they wanted to be involved with our project. Carmen and I conferred and agreed to invite Mark and Melissa to move into the 20th Street apartment. They were thrilled and moved in the next day. Eventually, Mark became our art director and Melissa, the comics editor. Miron never lived at 20th Street, but he was often there six to seven days a week helping out on the magazine. It wasn't long before the 20th Street flat became a constant meeting place for wide array of amazing artists, writers, and spiritual teachers from all over the Bay Area. Some came and went; others stayed for shorter or longer periods of time. Thus the *Magical Blend* commune was born.

In our second issue Mark Roland created an illustrative poem, which he called *Children of the Dream*. The first stanza read:

> The children of the dream awaken,
> Glistening and insane with glee
> The age of green in a golden land
> Where white horses dance
> In the palm of your hand.

In her comic, *Clodzilla in Poppy Land,* Melissa Snow Wind wrote:

> Part of the change you have already made,
> Self-realization has grown.
> The remaining tasks will not delay,
> And you are not alone.

And Miron Murcury stated in his *Elron* comic:

"In the early years at sea, Elron joined other animals in a successful adventure, being their own high school. Here, where ideas came alive, he found companionship."

To me these three excerpts were prophetic and best described the *Magical Blend* commune years.

With very little money and no idea of how to operate a business or distribute a magazine, we rallied the volunteers with a potluck, housewarming party. Here everyone met everyone else, encountering people they would never meet in their usual social circles. Tom Coulter, a staunch Republican, met Amber Faith, whom we had already designated as the artist for our second issue's cover. Amber had just moved to Marin from Wisconsin, where she had been a high priestess in a witch's coven. The ultra-conservative John Oberdorf became friends with the hippy visionary cartoonist Mark Roland. The exchange of information between these various characters was truly mind-boggling. Most people got drunk or high or both and then we had a New Age ceremony where everyone in the overstuffed apartment joined together to "Om" and visualize a great, successful future for the magazine. The first issue was getting great reactions from everyone who saw it, and the second issue was coming together even better. We invited everyone at the party to come over the following Saturday morning. We planned to break into teams and canvas the city, selling the first issue to whichever bookstores seemed interested and interesting.

Sales proved a difficult hurdle, especially for me, a true-blue anticapitalist if ever there was one. But I made the effort, convinced that getting our information out to a wider audience was worth the compromise. That Saturday, I hit the streets with Stephen Spears, a loyal volunteer and great comic artist/writer, whose self-improvement energy appeared in the form of comics, illustrations, or articles in most of our first 20 issues.

In an article from issue #7, Steven wrote, "As I had learned from the Silva Method of mind control, each of our lives are crafted by what we think. Our strongest thoughts usually attract a corresponding existence to us. The mind needs to be viewed as a muscle and we each need to develop our own tools to strengthen and focus it, to unfold the lives we really desire." Despite that quote and Steven's generally positive philosophy, that morning we were doubtful about our abilities as salesmen.

Our first stop was Gary Arlington's comic book store, located on 23rd Street in the Mission. I said, "Hi, I'm Michael. We published this magazine here in San Francisco. You . . . You . . . You don't want to sell any in your store do you?" Gary, who had encouraged many underground comic artists, said, "Sure, let me see it." I tripped on the floor handing him a copy. He took six and a salesman was born. The next week, Tom Coulter accompanied me down to Silicon Valley, where he helped me refine my sales approach at a number of new stores from Redwood City to San Jose.

Our first real distribution coup from those days came when City Lights, the famous Lawrence Ferlinghetti-owned beatnik bookstore where Jack Kerouac, Allen Ginsberg, and many others used to read poetry, agreed to take copies of *Magical Blend*. Even better, they displayed it in the front window with a sign "New San Francisco Magazine Debut." Many stores on Haight Street in the city, on Telegraph Avenue in Berkeley, and throughout Marin said they would sell it. None of them would pay us in advance, however, and given the discount structure that these stores worked under, we received only $0.75 from each store for each copy that they took. With the cost of bus tickets or gas, we calculated that we lost money on almost every store.

Yet we were undaunted. We rented a San Francisco post office box and one of us would take the bus down every day to retrieve the mail. There were usually two or three envelopes waiting for us. People began writing to ask how they might subscribe. We had to figure out a system for doing that. A few out-of-state stores wanted to sell copies; again, we had to devise a system. But most of the mail came from tons of artists, poets, and writers who wanted us to publish their creative efforts.

Robert Anton Wilson and the *Cosmic Trigger*

After the release and distribution of issue #1, the volunteer staff had a real, live magazine to show people. With this, we all began making many new contacts. Antro Allie, Verge and Jackie Belanger's highly creative author and occult teacher friend, had been taking a class at San Francisco State University from the wife of Robert Anton Wilson. Antro had actually met this famous author, who was responsible for great books like *The Illuminatus Trilogy* and *Cosmic Trigger*. He gave him a copy of the magazine. Bob was a prolific writer and offered to craft an article for our second issue if we would go by and pick it up. I was ecstatic. I went over to his home one morning with Stephen Spears.

Bob and his wife, Arlene, were staying in an apartment near the San Francisco State campus, close to the ocean. They were warm, friendly, inquisitive, and supportive. We were told that his books hadn't paid very well and that they were both very interested in getting out some information about how the world really operates. Some of Bob and Arlene's friends included people like Tim Leary, John Lilly, and Terence McKenna, and they offered to give them copies of our first issue and tell them that they should write for us as well. We talked while sharing coffee with cream and sugar. I could barely contain my excitement over meeting these brilliant people and their offer to tell others about us. Stephen and I stayed for about an hour, and then thanked them and said good-bye. We returned to 20th Street around 1 P.M. that afternoon. Several members of the staff were there, which was no surprise—several members of the staff were always there! We showed them Robert's great article and talked excitedly about some of the people that the Wilsons had offered to introduce us to.

Things had been hectic since the first issue came out, and we were setting up systems and defining what it actually was we were attempting to accomplish. We were way behind on much of the more tedious, detailed labor. But when I got back to the apartment that day, I felt inspired. My mind seemed crystal-clear and my energy was wonderfully balanced. Stephen felt that same way. We began to seriously hammer out some of our more difficult questions or problems. As we worked, most of the volunteers caught our enthusiasm and we all shared an extremely productive afternoon and evening.

By 11 P.M., all the volunteers had left, and two of my apartment-mates went to bed. Stephen and I were still feeling great—not speedy, not wired, not tired, just awake and inspired. We laughed together and kept working, amazed at our focus and concentration. We worked all night, got everything caught up, and even created some wonderful new systems that we used for years to come.

When the sun came up we were still going strong. After breakfast, a number of volunteers started coming by, and we explained what we had done and began making plans to increase circulation with the second issue. Again, we worked all day together. The rest of the volunteers all left about 6 P.M. Sunday. Stephen and I were a bit tired, so we went out to dinner. Afterward, he went home and I crashed for the evening. I slept just great with wonderful dreams.

The next morning, Stephen and I compared notes. We both had woken up at our regular time and felt pretty normal. However, we knew that something extraordinary had happened to us. I decided to call Bob Wilson to ask what he had put into our coffee and where I could purchase some. He said, "I hate to disappoint you but I don't know what you are talking about. I would never give anyone something without asking them first. Besides, I would never waste such a great substance as you describe on strangers! And, anyway, I don't buy or sell or do drugs. But we did enjoy meeting you and look forward to your second issue."

Stephen and I were both in disbelief. The energy had been so real! Possibly it was just a contact high from being in the presence of a "great man," or perhaps we were powered by a force from within ourselves. But I have always secretly suspected that Bob put something in our coffee cups that morning.

Witches and Parties

When the dust settled from our big housewarming party, the San Francisco area witches and pagans had all rallied to our cause in a big way. Apparently, we had become their new cause célèbre. We began attending teachings run by that well-known practitioner of the wiccan arts, Starhawk; we attended many different covens' rituals. And slowly but surely, at our weekly *Magical Blend* volunteer planning and working meetings, the witches began dominating.

With our communal home base set up on 20th Street, and momentum building after such a fine debut, we turned our attention toward creating our second issue. We wrote a letter to the spiritual and prolific author Shakti Gawain, care of her book publisher, to see if we could get her to write something for us on visualization. She called us back herself and invited us over to meet her and Mark Allen, who had done great astrology books and New Age music tapes. They were lovers and together they owned their own publishing company. What nice people—so friendly and generous. They used visualization and astrology and all these New Age tools to become rich and famous, but remained very nice and approachable. It was great to have their commitment to be in our second issue. In his article, Mark wrote about the effect and power of the moon energy as it passes through different astrological signs. The piece said, "The Moon's energy affects us on deep, subtle intuitive, and emotional levels. . . . Watching the moon tunes us into a monthly cycle and our emotional and intuitive cycles."

In her article, Shakti focused on the power of belief, desire, and expectations in manifesting the results we want in our lives. This is a basic set of tools that I still utilize regularly.

We were so excited about the presence of Shakti Gawain and Mark Allen in the magazine that we called up the publisher of Linda Clark, the leading expert on angels, and asked if she might write something for us as well. We got to talk with Linda but she declined to write something new; however, she was lovely and said we could use some of her writing from her latest book for free. In the piece we chose, she states powerfully, "Angels not only exist, if you just send out a call to a good angel to help with a problem, which you will no doubt state, the angel switchboard is said to get busy and summon the angel or angels you need to handle your particular problem." I have used this countless times and it works extremely well.

With those three names and Robert Anton Wilson, our second release looked to be another star-filled issue. In his piece, Wilson wrote, "When you have a goal that is noble enough to inspire you, it will be hedonistic enough (in the classic sense) to keep you amused; you will soon be too busy to worry about the naysayers and doom-mongers." This is still good advice. Issue #2 also featured an article on the basics of doing divination with Tarot cards. The article was written by a then-unknown author by the name of Mary Greer. Mary has since gone on to publish what are considered by many to be the world's best Tarot books. Today, she is renowned for her knowledge of the Tarot.

We had printed 20,000 copies of issue one and continued to use them as modular furniture. The boxes of fifty and 100 made great tables, chairs, and even couches. It was clear that we had been a touch over-optimistic with regard to potential distribution on that first issue, so we decided to print just 2,000 copies of issue #2. Our printer out in Sacramento agreed to do the job for $2,500. When we had gathered much more than 72 pages of what we felt was important, new, original, and transformative material, the volunteer team voted on what would go in, who would edit or touch up what, and which page it would go on. When we calculated the funds we had accumulated to that point, we had collected $1,729.57. Those of us most involved pitched in the difference. We had reached our goal—with almost $30 to spare! Thus, late in the fall of 1980, issue #2 of *Magical Blend* was born. The issue was heavy on the wiccan themes, but all in all it was a unique, wonderful, and magical collection of art and editorial.

After completing all the distribution work, we had a winter solstice party to celebrate getting a second issue out and to begin work on the third issue. It was at this party that we had our first extended family rift. The majority who attended were not pagan or witches. Although most everyone liked issue #2, many felt strongly that we had erred on the side of being too witchy. Everyone had their own agenda of what this new neophyte publication should become. The subgroup that lobbied the strongest was led by Dan Gold. Dan had brought an interesting and impressive fellow by the name of Ed Ellsworth to the party. Ed moved in moneyed circles and was then working with John Lilly, the renowned pioneer of interspecies communication, especially dolphins. Between them, Lou and Ed knew almost everyone that had done anything even somewhat related to cetaceans, whales, and dolphins. They made a strong case that if our third issue was dedicated exclusively to saving the whales and dolphins, they could get National Geographic photographers and artists to donate materials. They promised us tons of contributors, even articles from John Lilly and Jacques Cousteau. They even guaranteed we would sell all the magazines we printed at once and more because of the general interest and their contacts. Their pitch was quite impressive. We made the decision to do a "Save the Whales and

The Birth of *Magical Blend*—Issues 1–4 (1980–1981)

Dolphins" issue. This would lessen the witchy image that we had gotten, show the world that *Magical Blend* was capable of being many things, provide easy access to famous contributors, and maybe even pay for its own printing and postage costs. What could be better?

The Business

Within issue #2, we included subscription envelopes for the first time and raised the cover price to $3.00. Then we raided the local Cala supermarket, taking all the cardboard boxes and brown paper bags we could carry back to the apartment. Every volunteer was asked to bring tape to the weekly meeting. We cut up the boxes and bags and then retaped them. Those bookstores that we couldn't easily reach by bus or car received shipments in these custom-sized boxes. Those people who had subscribed after issue #1 received their copies in brown paper bag packages—every bit as good as envelopes and at a great price.

The next day we returned to Cala in the cold rain and borrowed some shopping carts. We filled them up with our bundles and pushed them 12 blocks to the post office, where we waited in line and mailed our expensive mountain of magazines. We then returned the carts and went home to warm up around the kitchen stove. The only heater in the apartment was broken and electric heaters are too expensive when you are spending all your money on magazine printing and postage.

Just before the end of 1980, Carmen and I got a miraculous deal on a last-minute, ridiculously cheap, six-city airline ticket. We decided to stop in Los Angeles, Chicago, Boston, New York, Miami, and Negril, Jamaica (where my brother, Spider, who had contributed an article to our first two issues, lived during the winter in most years). The stated purpose of our trip was to find magazine distributors. However, it was during this time traveling alone together that Carmen and I realized that we had fallen in love. Consummating our relationship was like the realization of my dreams, fears, and fantasies. We had always joked as to which one of us was the better lover, and we had great enjoyment attempting to find out.

In each city, we would look up the local magazine distributors in the yellow pages, call them up, and make an appointment to show them our two issues of *Magical Blend*. We were extremely successful and found five distributors who agreed to sell issues #2 and #3, as well as all future issues as we printed them. In Los Angeles we picked up the Armadillo Trading Company; in Chicago, Homing Pigeon Distributors; in Boston, Somerville Distributors; in New York, Ubiquity Distribution; and in Miami, The Herald Force. We even found a couple of tourist bookstores in Negril that agreed to carry us. After five successful weeks of traveling, staying in low budget hotels and with friends and family, we were glad to get back to the commune, where we moved into the same bedroom at last.

Issue #3 was a long time in the making, taking more than half of 1981! In the apartment, we played Paul Horn's whale songs continuously. We read everything available on the subject of cetaceans. We hitchhiked from Oregon to San Diego to meet people, gather information, increase circulation, and attempt to raise money.

We hadn't realized how much the pagan community had done to help get issue #2 out. We had to reinvent the volunteer structure and find all new material for *Magical Blend*. We had fundraising parties throughout the year and a wide array of people came. Jeff Chandler, a cover artist for *Omni Magazine*, whose art had also been used by Disney and *Scientific American*, came to one party and met a women visiting from Denmark. They fell in love and got married within a month. The first of many *Magical Blend* marriages.

The parties usually provided enough contributions to pay for themselves but didn't raise much money for printing. By October of 1981, we had received the promised articles from John Lilly, his wife Toni Lilly, and Jacques Cousteau. We had gathered unique and high quality comics, poems, stories, and interviews dealing with whales and dolphins. Issues #1 and #2 had no interviews. Doing our first ones was a new learning experience. We drove in a borrowed car to Jim Nollen's house on the beach north of Marin. Jim was famous for using music to communicate with orcas. Jerry, Jeff Fletcher, Carmen, and I introduced ourselves. Then I said, "We have a tape recorder but we have never interviewed anyone. Do you know what we should do?" Jim laughed and led us through the process of interviewing him. In the process of researching the issue, I got to swim with John Lilly and his research dolphins. I also got the military to tell me that all their research was restricted from news media access.

When it came time for printing, we had saved up $1,550 from contributions, donations, and earnings from bookstores and subscribers. However, we needed $3,200 to print 3,000 copies. We wanted to print more but we didn't have enough for that and #2 was almost sold out. Those of us most involved donated what we could to make up the difference. In November of 1981, we finally printed issue #3, featuring a fantastic Dan Gold cover. It was like nothing we had ever done before.

The response was mixed. Issue #2 had gotten us received by many metaphysical, occult, and wiccan stores. Many of those were not thrilled with #3 and let us know about it. We didn't have many subscribers but many of them wrote to say they hadn't expected what they received. Yet the issue did bring in new subscribers and Last Gasp Comic Distributors finally agreed to distribute us.

We did the mailing for issue #3 much in the same way that we did it for #2, only with more shopping carts, boxes, bags, and bigger postal bills. We actually used that same procedure, modified just a bit, until issue #14, when we just couldn't do it by ourselves anymore. From that point until now, subscribers received their copies directly from our printer.

In October of 1981, I got to fulfill a lifelong dream when I met Buckminster Fuller. He was one feisty old man! He said that if we wanted to interview him, we should dedicate the entire issue to him and his ideas. "I will be dead soon and we're trying to save the world," he continued. "Don't you want to help more than just an article?" The theme for issue #3 had been rather difficult, limiting, and not as great for sales as we had hoped, so we politely refused his offer. We did feature a great interview with him in #4, however. Bucky was just so very brilliant and such an inspiration. I always wished we had done that Bucky theme, for he did die a few years later and I feel that his work was extremely important and has been mostly overlooked since his death.

Around that time, I also got to speak at length on the phone with Marilyn Ferguson. I was seeking her permission to reprint part of her great book, *The Aquarian Conspiracy*. Some day I hope to write a book that changes the way people think as much as she did with that one. For the three years following its release, it was the spiritual book that everyone quoted. I remember Ms. Ferguson as being quite eloquent, brilliant, and caring. You could tell she was busy with countless important demands on her time, but she never tried to rush me. It was awesome to think of the people I was coming into contact with!

About that time, we had a booth at the Haight Street fair. There we met Van Ault, a literary witch and head warlock of a gay New Age witches' coven in Tennessee. He wrote a great little article for #4, entitled, "Sharing and Supply," in which he spoke eloquently about the power our thoughts have in affecting reality not only for ourselves, but for all of humanity. He ends it by saying, "The source of lack, as espoused in the concept of inflation, is the same as the source of unemployment, hunger, illness, and loneliness. Only through the sharing of our being will the supply of this world be released, fully distributed, and enjoyed by all the world's people, for all of us it was intended." Van's writing was always this thought provoking, and he continued to give us great material for many issues afterward. He was a hard working, tireless volunteer who added much to *Magical Blend*.

This issue was typeset and laid out at night at the office where Jerry worked during the day. We all snuck in after hours and used the facilities. But because we were sneaking about, people got locked in stairwells and outside in the rain for hours! The day after we were all done Jerry called me at 8 A.M. and said, "Michael! Quick get dressed and get down here. We left the layout boards here and if they find them I'll be fired!" I jumped on a bus, went in, said "Hi" to Jerry's boss, gave Jerry a package of apples (all I could think of as an excuse to bring), and scooped up the boards without being noticed.

Issue #4 was a big leap forward for *Magical Blend*. In it we had interviews, black and white pictures, a dolphin article, a witchcraft article, poetry, comics, and lots of New Age magic. We also created our first four-color cover. We had met a famous poster designer, Gilbert Johnson, who had done many Haight Street posters back in the 1960s. He explained to us how we could use mechanical overlays to basically hand construct very detailed four-color negatives without having to pay the then-exorbitant color separation fees. The most artistic and detail-oriented volunteers sat for days working on these hand separated overlays. I did things like get coffee, beer, wine, and joints. I also attempted to put on page numbers only to have them all have to be redone because they were crooked. Oh well! I was and am a writer and a leader, not a fine detail artist.

The Magic

Magic was never far beneath the surface of everything that we did. One night around this time, we called a meeting of the staff in order to try to manifest extended success for our publication. Present were Carmen, Jeff Fletcher, Steven Spears, Jerry Snider, Melissa Snow Wind, Mark Roland, and me. We gathered in a circle, om'ed, and spoke words of ritual calling in the four directions and the spirit of the magazine, as well as any and all spiritual entities or powers who would listen and take effect. We created a dome of power to surround us. Then we each passed around the talking stick. We were all to speak magically and powerfully as we held this stick, in hopes that we could manifest the best possible future for the magazine. As the stick went around and around, the transformative magic built. Then there was a loud crack. We were no longer in the room. We had entered the dimension of manifestation. It was as if we sat in the center of the universe where all that exists is given birth. We were blown ferociously by our beliefs and hopes. We intoned together that the magazine would grow and evolve to help transform the whole planet and cocreate the golden age. There was an entity that appeared and disappeared quickly. She seemed to be connected to the essences or manifesting energies of the magazine. We asked that issue #5 would have a four-color separated cover and that every issue thereafter would improve. We then broke the spell and returned in shock to our living room.

All things have spirits! Often, strong spirits that live in the formless void develop an intent to create something for their spirit to inhabit, evolve, and animate. I believe that *Magical Blend* magazine is one of those things. First, there was a powerful spirit. She roamed the Earth observing, inspiring, and assisting in the growth and spiritual development of humanity and the planet. At a point in the late 1970s, this spirit began making a plan. It wanted to have a physical means to communicate with people; to spread ideas and stretch minds, to open hearts and to shine light into dark, shadowy, and fear-filled places. It is obvious to me why this spirit chose San Francisco as the place to come into being. San Francisco is a hotbed of creativity, tolerance, and experimentation. It is a magnet that draws rebellious, creative, and nonconformist people to the area. However, why the spirit chose me to be its front man has always been a bit unclear to me. I have always felt blessed to have been chosen and honored to be given much of the credit for what I knew to be this spirit entity's will and works. I have always attempted to do my best with the resources that I have been given.

I also work closely with the spirits of the Incan gods and goddesses and sometimes these forces have conflicting desires of me. This pushes me to make difficult choices. I've never known why this entity chose me instead of a rich, experienced publishing executive or a beautiful, well-connected socialite, but the opportunity has always made me feel quite blessed. Why me instead of an already famous author, sports figure, or movie star? It confuses me still. Yet spirits have their own vision of how they want things to be.

In the early years, I was aware of this spirit yet unsure if it was my imagination or just some sort of a wish. As the years have turned into decades, I have become quite clear that the spirit of *Magical Blend* is a real entity, and has been one long before there was a being by the name of Michael Peter Langevin. I have spoken with the spirit often in dreams and prayers. She often appears to me as the girl on our first issue's cover, and almost as often as the women on the cover of issue #7. She has also appeared to me as a tree, a dog, a dragonfly, and a crow, among other forms. Sometimes she appears as a gentle, whispering message. She comes to me most often when I am overwhelmed, depressed, confused, or exhausted. I guess those are the times I need her encouragement most. I often ask her why she allows it to be so difficult a process. Why has *Magical Blend* seldom made much money for prolonged periods of time? Why doesn't she assist more with distribution growth or even advertising sales? Why doesn't she send me more staff or employees who stay longer? Why hasn't she made me a millionaire or even allowed me to rest much? She laughs and radiates unconditional love. She smiles and usually says something like, "It is as much your choice as mine. If you had the same staff and guaranteed circulation growth and a secure base of advertising income, it would get stale. It would fall into a formula. It would lose its edge. The days are coming when all of that would be right. However until then trust in my vision and my decisions. Trust in your own inner guidance. Remember how many people our magazine has touched and inspired and helped through all these years. How many people have opened their hearts and improved their lives because of what we have created. If one prisoner decided to change their ways because of *Magical Blend*, if one sick person decided to heal, if one fear-filled person decided to love and take chances, would not all your suffering, struggles, and hard work be worthwhile? You know many are living better lives because they read *Magical Blend* magazine."

Until now, we were supposed to be a well-kept secret being bought and read by only those who were ready for it. Circulation had to stay just as big as we could manage and we had to have limited funds so that it would be focused, refined, and dedicated to unique reinvention on a regular basis. Today, we have published nearly 100 issues that are extremely different from each other and any other publication that has ever been printed. That is wealth and accomplishment beyond compare. I have been allowed a loving wife, wonderful children, a farm with horses, and work that I love. That too is wealth. Perhaps the time is right for me to now become a millionaire and a famous author and public speaker; if not, then it's because I'm not ready and neither is the planet. These next ten years are when we can all make our greatest impact in the future of humanity. Will it be easy? Ha! Will the stakes be raised and the challenges and victories become grander? Yes!

Speaking with spirits who have chosen you and decided to use you as one of their chess pieces seems to be something I do in this life. The spirit of *Magical Blend* is different than that of the Inca goddesses and gods I have known. She is powerful, yet not a goddess, and she is more evolved than any humans I have known, with supernatural powers and abilities. Yet I sense her frustrations, her limitations, her hopes, and her fears. She cries and strives for humanity and the Earth. She enjoys the experiences she has. She is a wonderful, unconditionally loving, sensual spirit entity. Yet she has a mission and is totally committed to it and to having it done her way. She chose me, loves me, helps me, and yet is not often there for me when I could use her assistance. Even when she assists it is seldom in the ways I would desire her to. We work together and seem to have similar goals, yet we are resistant allies always working for a compromise to serve both us and our mission. I am honored and blessed that she chose me. Yet I resist and resent her as well.

A business can begin in many ways. Some start with lots of knowledge, experience, and investment money. I have seen countless magazines and businesses of all sorts come and go during these last 25 years. The ones that have survived and prospered didn't have to have anything but a vision, a dream, enthusiasm, and the will to do whatever it takes to make things work. That's *Magical Blend.* Money is a great reward; however, in and of itself it doesn't usually create success nor maintain it. I believe that *Magical Blend* came into being not only because of the guiding spirit, not only because of its uniqueness, and not even because I have worked so hard for so many years (but I do believe that helped greatly). *Magical Blend* magazine has survived, evolved, and prospered because it gives people the inspiration to improve their lives. That has been the dream and the vision from the beginning. Many people spend most of their time worrying and concentrating on what's wrong in their lives. Our thoughts are far more powerful than most people realize. *Magical Blend* reminds people to focus on what they want to happen. We advise people to concentrate on what is working and what feels right. I know that this vision, along with many people's blood, sweat, and tears, has made *Magical Blend* the successful, internationally distributed publication that it is today. And that, to me, is the truest, purest form of magic that anyone could ever hope to experience.

THREE

WHERE DID EVERYONE GO?—
ISSUES 5–12 (1982–1985)

Changes

Through our first two years, essentially the same group of people worked on *Magical Blend*. By the start of 1982, the magazine had passed beyond its initial stage of awkwardness and begun to mature into a more professional publication. But then, just as things were coming together in a way that I had once only dreamed about, things changed. Some very important people made the decision to leave the magazine. Others came aboard to replace them, bringing unique insights and different creative abilities. The magazine and the mission adjusted to these changes in our world, not for the first time, and not for the last.

But much of that change was still in our future. As 1982 began, most of the earlier team was still together, and dedicated to making *Magical Blend* the best magazine it could be. We decided that issue #5 needed a four-color painting for the cover. This felt very important to all of us. It was absolutely imperative that we be able to find affordable ways to appear professional. We wanted this issue to represent who we had become and where we were headed. As a group, we asked Mark Roland to paint a visionary picture, with great detail, showing a timeless city. The intention was that this mystical city could be taken for Atlantis of the lost past or interpreted as some future Utopia.

Mark was excited. However, he would only agree to spend the countless hours required to create such a painting if we promised to run the cover without any cover lines, only the price and logo. In addition, Mark requested that we order an overrun of the cover with neither a logo nor a price. We agreed.

The next week, I was invited to a predawn ceremony celebrating Project Artue, a converted factory in the Mission District only a half a mile from the *Magical Blend* commune. Many writers, artists, and computer wizards were renting space there. Antro Allie once wrote and performed a play in the main theater complex. On this day, there was to be a showing of visionary artwork at sunrise, appropriately themed "Transition." I had to get there at 4:30 A.M. and the ceremony would be followed by a wine and cheese breakfast. The ceremony was wonderful (I love genuinely creative ceremonies). The art was good and bad, but only half the artists could get up that early. So I guess I got to meet and speak with the healthiest ones, or at least the ones who were the most driven. I also found myself talking with many agents and gallery owners. This led me to Lazaris, in the form of Jack Pursel. Jack was the owner of a visionary gallery in Marin and he channeled an entity claiming to be ancient and all-wise, who was referred to by the name of Lazaris. He was hunting for creative low cost ways to promote some of his artists. I asked if he had color separations of their work. In fact, he did, some of which he felt would look good at 8¹/₂ by 11 inches or smaller. I asked how he would feel about us printing them and crediting his gallery and printing contact info.

He was enthusiastic. Jack agreed to let us use up to five pieces an issue. He also recommended a printer in North Carolina who would print four-color almost as cheaply as black and white as long as we supplied the negatives. So, we now had a deal. He even had a friend who owed him a favor for color separation work, so we were able to affordably and professionally separate Mark Roland's cover.

Issue #5 was another big step forward for us; it looked great and was filled with compelling editorial. We all gave our best efforts and then some. It was by far the best issue we had crafted to date. However, after this issue came out, it was clear that the relationship between Carmen and me was over. Disagreements and arguments about what should go in each issue and how everything should be done took a major toll on our relationship. To leave no doubt about the finality of our breakup, she moved in with Dan Gold. Meanwhile, Jerry was just plain exhausted. He was thinking of quitting, partially because Carmen was losing interest, and partially because it was just so darn much work with no compensation. I talked both of them into taking a one-issue break while I did a comics and poetry issue with our still enthusiastic volunteers.

The volunteers at that time happened to be some of the best people that ever worked on *Magical Blend*. Jeff Fletcher, Steven Spears, Verge Belanger, Miron Murcury, Joe Blondo, and Melissa Snow Wind were a fine, talented, and diverse group. We also had some great newcomers helping us by that time. Arwin and Wendy, a couple of artist/poet hippies, would drive 75 miles two and three times a week, from Santa Rosa, to add their unique skills to the magazine. They both drew some amazing mandala art. Wendy was the granddaughter of Alistair Crowley himself, so she knew a great deal about magic and had been told many fascinating stories from her grandmother. Qalbi and Hillary were another lovely couple who had become important players in our world as well. Qalbi was heavily into meditation and would spend whole weeks doing his very unique line art. Hillary was a healer and a masseuse who supported them both and did some nice writing, too. They seldom missed a volunteer meeting or work party and both added a great amount to our organization. Then there was Vince Emery, who had written a best-selling book on the coming Internet revolution but liked being around funky artist types with high ideals. He always had great suggestions like, "Let's sell our inventory of back issues—I bet we can get $15.00 apiece for all these #1s!"

All these volunteers were extremely talented, but I had no skilled lieutenants without Jerry or Carmen. The rest of us pushed forward regardless, sure that New Age comics would sell big. I even had fantasies of launching a New Age comics line. I guess change at *Magical Blend* was in the air, for at that time Mark Roland and Melissa also broke up and Mark moved out of the 20th Street commune. The lovely Bonnie Blackwell, who was a radio broadcaster, and her brilliant husband Mick, an impressionistic and poetic artist and childcare worker, rented our extra rooms upstairs. Bonnie and Mick unofficially joined the extended *Magical Blend* family. Melissa made friends with Anne Hiddenone, a talented and determined young lady with an English degree who was eager to get involved with *Magical Blend*. Soon, Anne and her boyfriend Roy Kong had moved into the second floor. We also made room for Mick Blackwell's brothers James and Todd and their good friend Karie, a Japanese exchange student studying art. Todd was a wilderness adventure trip leader, and James a dynamic coffee service salesman.

The 20th Street commune was full of people, creativity, energy, and, of course, magic. At its peak, our loosely defined commune consisted of us renting the entire three-story building and sixteen to twenty people living there. We would have meetings up to five times a week where we all sat in a circle and used a talking stick in the Native American tradition to specify who could talk. You could only hold the stick for five minutes at max. Then it was someone else's turn. All decisions for the building and the magazine were made in this fashion or by majority vote, which could be frustrating. When things were at one particularly low point, I do remember losing it. My grandfather's ring (a family heirloom), many of my favorite books, and all my personal food had disappeared, with no one taking responsibility. I stood up with the talking stick and yelled, "I am tired of this communal shit! I am tired of the opinion that what is yours is yours and what is mine is yours also!" And with that I passed the stick and sat down. Things changed for the better soon thereafter.

During the years between 1980 and 1983, an issue would usually come together over a series of late nights and weekends. Most decisions for issues one through ten were made by whomever was available to do the work. An average issue could take us anywhere from three to nine months to complete, print, and ship. After an issue was sent to the printer, we would have weekly meetings on whatever night it seemed most people would be able to attend. Around seven o'clock, we would all gather in the largest available room. We would sit in a circle and begin with a group ritual and visualization. Then we would begin passing the talking stick. To decide on articles, art portfolios, and cover artists, we passed the talking stick, listened to each other, and voted. It was the same for themes, numbers of copies to print, large expenditures—on everything that *Magical Blend* did, we passed the talking stick and let everyone have their say.

Of course, my role as copublisher and loudest leader was to make these decisions manifest. I also made the decisions that couldn't wait until the upcoming meeting, taking advice from anyone who was available at the time. I often had to explain these decisions at length to the group at the next meeting. As we got closer to the day that the issue was to be sent to the printer, our weekly meetings began to be supplanted by weekend work sessions. We would spend much of Friday night and all of Saturday and Sunday editing, doing layouts, and pasting up the issue. In those days, without wonderful things like computers, this was difficult and time-consuming work that would usually take about three intense weekends. My role was to coordinate the work flow, to assist in decisions, and to make sure that everyone was working on task and that their needs were met.

Realignment

But even all of this excitement and activity couldn't take my mind off the things that were troubling me. I was devastated when Carmen fell out of love with me. I was confused, crushed, lonely, and depressed, with tremendous amounts of self-doubt and feelings of invalidity thrown in for good measure. Her moving in with Dan Gold only added to my devastation.

Once again, years later, I have come to understand some of the important lessons that relationships often offer us. Specifically, Carmen and I shared many aspects of our lives for a few years as close friends and co-workers. This was followed by a time as intense and passionate lovers, during which time we shared the major responsibility in attempting to lead *Magical Blend* and coordinate a commune of creative eccentrics. In addition, we were both working full time in a variety of demanding jobs because *Magical Blend* barely had enough money to cover its bills, much less pay us or any of the others who worked on it ceaselessly. In fact, many of the volunteers often donated their own money to make ends meet.

Carmen and I seldom shared time alone except the hours we shared in making love or sleeping. If we had any time alone together we were in bed. We never thought to make time for examining, developing, or evolving our relationship. I think that Carmen just got tired of never just being able to share simple things like a movie without one of us talking about decisions which affected increasing numbers of lives. It seemed that whenever we were together, we had important decisions to make, compromise over, or argue about. It got so intense that we would interrupt our ecstatic tantric rituals to discuss what should be on page ten of the next issue. That level of constant intensity tends to wear people down over a prolonged period of time, and in our case ruined a most unique and wonderful relationship.

I had quit my bartending job a few months before and was then working at an agency which provided temporary shelter for runaway and beaten girls. I was working around the clock from Sunday at 8 A.M. until Tuesday at noon. When I wasn't at work, instead of exploring the meaning of what had been the nature of my relationship with Carmen or why she had felt compelled to leave me, I took to avoiding that kind of soul searching altogether, as well as the pain of the loss.

I filled the hours when I wasn't working, at the shelter or on *Magical Blend,* by riding the buses around San Francisco and meeting women. If they seemed interesting or sensual or fun I would ask them out for a drink. Maybe half of them told me to go to hell. Oh, well. However, if they said yes, then I would see where things might lead. I was just attempting to lose myself and overcome my self-doubt and feelings of failure. I wasn't looking for another long-term relationship. I did see some of the women a few times, and we generally ended up having great sex. It wasn't necessarily the healthiest approach to healing from a failed relationship, but eventually I started getting over the pain of losing Carmen's love.

The changing nature of my major relationships, friendships, and living situation offered quite the growing experience. The coming together of issue #6 in 1982 proved to be my crutch and my symbolic crossing of the valley of the shadow of death.

The volunteers and I decided that we would throw ourselves into creating the most unique and poetic New Age comic book ever printed. This was the goal and this is what I used to keep myself focused and on track. But it wasn't easy. Much of that time I was doubt-ridden and fearful, sure that I would fail without Carmen and Jerry, as well as William Stewart and Mark Roland, both of whom also left around this time. I didn't feel that I could do it with just the talented volunteers that remained. I sometimes felt as though I couldn't do anything.

Eventually, I pulled myself together by reminding myself that the difference between doing something and not doing it is just doing it. We all have fears and doubts, but great people acknowledge them and then use them as catalysts to help them do what needs to be done. I had always landed on my feet before, for I was a magician. One of my burning goals was to become a powerful magic worker. I dreamed of being an equal to Merlin and Gandalf and the comic book master of the mystical arts, Dr. Strange. I had spoken with the Inca gods and goddesses, and I had been told by cosmic beings that I had important work to do. I had to believe that I could do whatever I decided to focus my intent on. At the very least, I could cocreate a *Magical Blend* comic book with the assistance, hard work, and talents of the volunteer staff.

I decided that I would enjoy my life, and that together we all would make issue #6 a unique success. I decided that I would be better for my losses. Being mugged in New York's Central Park as a young man hadn't killed me. Being brutalized and nearly killed in Mexico hadn't killed me, either. I had had many relationships end before, and I always continued to enjoy life and come out ahead. This time would be no different. I decided I would just up my risk factor and push my envelope a bit more. I didn't want to die with an incomplete report card. I was willing to fail and make mistakes; that's the role of all brave and creative people. I was like the best metal, which has to pass through the hottest portion of the refining furnace. I would redefine my goals and my way of living life and I would more fully enjoy every experience I could have.

I took to going to jazz clubs and listening to the music until closing time. I experimented with altering my sleeping patterns. I attended many new and different spiritual groups and events in the greater Bay Area. And I met new women.

I will always remember coming home to the apartment one night with a date. At my kitchen table sat Verge Belanger, looking very gnomelike, Jeff Fletcher, looking very werewolflike, and

Steven Spears, looking very elflike. I introduced everyone and then my date and I went to bed. After a lovely sexual interlude, she was tired and wanted to sleep. Once she drifted off, I got up, went out to the living room, and worked with my good friends on the comics issue until the sun came up in the morning. Then my new friend and I enjoyed each other some more. What a strange, exotic, bohemian time it was for me.

We got issue #6 to the printer in September of 1982. The response to every issue had been mixed. However the response to issue #6 was the most extreme yet. Some stores stopped carrying us altogether after the issue came out. Some subscribers also wrote to say they hadn't expected and weren't crazy about a comics issue. Although there were some positive comments, most who contacted us were not pleased.

In hindsight, I think that this issue succeeded in being just what we had attempted to create, but unfortunately, no one quite knew what to make of it. There have not been very many poetic, New Age comic books ever printed anywhere. So this one was something unique and in some eyes wonderful but unsuccessful in finding a large receptive audience. Last Gasp sold a record number of copies—not enough to make up for the loss of sales at other outlets, but encouraging nonetheless. This issue also moved us, rather inadvertently, into the social circle of San Francisco's world-renowned underground comics artists. We were invited to their parties and homes. We got to know R. Crumb (who had created "Keep on Truckin'"), Trinie Robbins ("Love and Rockets"), and Sheldon ("The Fabulous Furry Freak Brothers").

In the fall of 1982, I went back to New England to visit family and friends. It had been a while since I had been back home, time during which I experienced a great many changes and personal evolution. I was shocked, however, to see that many of my old comrades had already decided how their lives were going to be. They hadn't seemed to have changed much during the preceding five years.

I returned to San Francisco with a renewed commitment to grow, change, and evolve throughout the rest of my life. But I had to make a statement. I was about to turn 30 and that seemed old. So I decided to do something radical, something that would make a statement about my willingness to change and experiment with different ways. I decided to get a blue mohawk. I went to a punk hairdresser and she took the entire afternoon to make my transformation complete. I went back to the 20th Street commune and everyone there freaked out. We were having a meeting that night. I walked in with my new haircut and attempted to do my leadership thing. Miron Murcury stood up and demanded, "Who are you and what are you doing trying to take charge?" Everyone broke down in laughter. I explained myself and the reasons behind my new image. Everyone was amused.

Jeff Fletcher thought that I had hit on a good idea, so he decided to dye his long hair fluorescent orange. That weekend was the New Age Renaissance Fair in San Jose. Jeff and I were the two who were manning the *Magical Blend* booth. People were either confused, bothered, angry, or amused by our appearance. We sold many magazines but other vendors wouldn't buy advertising from punks. When the next issue was delivered, I hopped into a borrowed car and set out on my regular delivery route. No one recognized me and most were uncomfortable receiving the magazine from me. I didn't get as many timely payments as usual for issues sold, either. I kept the mohawk for about three months and then I cut it off. It just wasn't good for business.

End or Beginning?

By the early spring of 1983, it became clear that issue #6 hadn't sold well on most newsstands or even most comic book stores. My dreams of a comics line crashed and burned.

However, good things began happening on other fronts. Anne Hiddenone, a new volunteer, turned out to be a great addition. She was very excited to be working on *Magical Blend,* and she had the skills necessary to handle editorial decisions. It was agreed that she would guest edit issue #7, with a health-oriented theme. Jerry and Carmen felt that they could handle her editorial pace better than mine, so they both agreed to come back. The four of us soon began to have regular meetings to discuss themes, edits, layouts, and designs.

We were so successful with our health-themed issue #7, with Anne as guest editor, that we thought we might dedicate our next issue to the theme of peace. We again reached out for a guest editor, asking one of the founders of the famous 1960s underground newspaper, the *Haight Street Oracle,* to perform the honors for issue #8. As events unfolded, this developed into a war-torn project the likes of which we had never seen before—rather ironic for an issue centered on peace!

Our guest editor had rather devolved from the 1960s. He had become anti-everything! He was able to convince many famous people to write very negative, critical, and depressing articles about the military-industrial complex, politics, religion, the environment, and life in general, none of which jibed with the positive, uplifting, and inspirational message that we always sought to portray in *Magical Blend.* We felt strongly that ours was a positive magazine about building alternative possibilities, not attacking what existed or even giving any energy to negative thoughts. We believed as a group that what people concentrated on grew in the world, so why focus on all that was wrong and not offer viable alternatives? Our idea of a peace issue was articles about positive actions people could take in their lives and in the world to make a difference, but that was nothing like the articles that our guest editor was bringing in.

During this period, we had volunteer meetings two or three times a week, which always ended with compromises that were unsatisfying for everyone. Eventually, at one meeting, our guest editor stood up and said, "I am tired of getting all this great material and having you reject it just because you have printed seven issues and have a readership. Either give me the freedom to include what I want how I want or I will withdraw all my materials and I will find another magazine to print them."

Now this represented about nine-tenths of the issue. We were down to the finish line after months of impossible meetings. This felt reminiscent of the first issue's ultimatums by Renaldo and Maria. However, this time, we put it to a vote of the volunteers. The decision was taken that he either abide by the group's agreements and let us approve the last two articles or the guest editorship was terminated. The spirit of *Magical Blend* seems not to like ultimatums. The guest editor took his articles, interviews, art, and photos and left in a huff. We all breathed a sigh of relief and began to work on a generic #8. It came together quickly and was printed in record time. I had to write diplomatic rejection letters to several famous people, but we had stood by our principles. As far as I know none of our guest editor's articles were ever printed anywhere.

Once that was done and the dust had settled, Carmen asked to have her name remain on the masthead even though she would not be very involved in the magazine while she decided what she was going to do with her life. She and Dan hadn't lived together long before Carmen decided to move down to Ojai, just north of Los Angeles. There, she lived in a spiritual shamanic commune led by a famous author, Joan Halifax, who had written the very popular book *Shamanic Wisdom*. I got to know Joan and learned much shamanic knowledge and ritual from her. She even agreed to write an article for us on shamanic healing.

It was tricky to have Carmen active with the magazine while living so far away, for she couldn't possibly help with the day-to-day organization. Therefore, I was grateful when Jerry agreed to reinvest and reinvolve himself fully with *Magical Blend*. It was decided that Jerry would become the associate publisher. In essence, this was another step towards him and me becoming partners in owning and operating *Magical Blend*. However, it was still a communal entity and even the financial costs were reported on many people's taxes at the time.

At about that time, I met Tara Kilpatrick, a social worker and graduate student who had moved to San Francisco from Evergreen, Colorado. Tara loved dolphins, was very warm, generous, and creative, and was good with money, too. We hit it off magically. She was so different from any women I had met that we began dating, and soon thereafter, she moved into the *Magical Blend* commune. She was very much involved with the magazine for the year that we were together.

A friend of *Magical Blend* at the time was a grower and seller of psilocybin mushrooms for fun and profit. At her urging we decided to have a party to celebrate the release of issue #8. It was then that I received a telephone call from my mother. My sister Pat had experienced a nervous breakdown while living with my Mom and my younger sister Elizabeth in San Diego. Liz and Mom had had to make the difficult decision to have Pat hospitalized. She had been diagnosed as having bipolar disorder. Tara realized that I was devastated by this phone call. She said, "I have a car and some money. Let's go get your sister out of the hospital and bring her to live with us in the *Magical Blend* commune. I just know that we can heal her." So off we went, driving Tara's little yellow Toyota down to San Diego. There we consoled my mother and sister Liz and checked Pat out of the psychiatric hospital. Tara and I were confident that the *Magical Blend* community could heal anything or anyone. I will always remember driving across the Bay Bridge late that night with Tara and Pat. The radio was playing and we were all singing along to the words of the great reggae singer Jimmy Cliff: "You can get it if you really want, but you must try, try, and try, try, and try. You'll succeed at last!"

That night, we moved Pat into one of the rooms on the first floor. She met all the communal members and joined in our insanity of preparing for the big party. We had sent invitations to all of our Bay Area friends, subscribers, contributors, bookstore owners, and acquaintances. It was a potluck and we just bought some alcohol and food and cleaned up everything when the big day came. The magic mushroom grower decided it was time to be generous with her crop. As people arrived at the party, any that wanted some were given a dose of magic mushrooms.

We always centered our parties around rituals to use the joyous group energy to envision and cocreate the best possible of shared futures for *Magical Blend* and all people touched by it. This time, Van Ault led us in burning a sacrificial copy of issue #8 in a cauldron in order to send its energies all over the world. Then San Francisco's infamous Sisters of Perpetual Indulgence performed as only they could—an outrageous ceremony that I will leave to the reader's imagination. Then we took a page from one of Starhawk's witchcraft books and did a spiral dance, joined with group chanting and loud affirmations.

The energies were way beyond description. Up on the roof sat the Blackwell family—Bonnie, her husband, Mick, and his brothers James and Todd. Todd had taken a few too many doses of mushrooms and the ceremony pushed him over the edge of sanity. He had a break with reality. He was quiet about it, though, and the party went on and on until about noon on the next day. When the last guest left, the *Magical Blend* commune was faced with the reality of having thrown an awesomely unique party that put us on the map in many people's minds.

Yet the fact remained that we now had two relatives living with us who actually belonged in psychiatric hospitals. For months verging on a year we had meetings, putting together issues #9 and #10 and attempting to heal Todd and Pat as best we could.

Happily, my sister Pat did eventually get better with lots of support, proper therapy, and medication. Todd, however, continued to get worse. He took to leaving messages on *Magical Blend's* answering machine saying, "Jesus loves you. God loves you. You must remember that they are the only true spiritual path. Please give up your evil and false New Age beliefs." When I put a stop to that, he took to inviting every street person he met to live in our commune. They would drink our cologne and perfumes. He would make them stews and soups with the weirdest combinations of food you have ever seen. That's when I finally told him that he could not invite anyone else into our house. I patiently explained that we could not house and feed all of San Francisco's homeless. He accused me, the commune, and the magazine of being selfish, greedy, and untrue to our stated values. From there it got even worse. I started doubting my own sanity. Many volunteers stopped attending meetings. I was so distracted that I got into a serious car accident. I wasn't hurt but the person I hit was. Eventually, I was forced to ask Todd to move out. I felt that to maintain any of my sanity and my ability to salvage any of my life or the magazine's existence, he had to go. He lived on the street for a month before he was hospitalized. This led to his being committed and eventually placed in a halfway treatment house, where he finally got the treatment he needed to heal.

About that time, my sister Pat and Todd's relatives all moved out. Tara and I broke up, and she too left the apartment. After their departure, I was alone on the third floor of the once crazy *Magical Blend* commune. I decided that I needed that luxury for the summer and fall. I moved the *Magical Blend* office back up to the third floor. Jeff Fletcher found some new roommates to move into the first floor, but they wanted nothing to do with a commune or *Magical Blend*. During that period, we had only sporadic meetings. I spent much of that summer and fall by myself, which was somewhat refreshing. I took this time to attempt to regather myself and realign my goals.

In October of 1983, without much effort, I applied for and was offered a well-paid position as a supervisor at Fred Finch, a treatment facility for emotionally disturbed teenagers. This was a great boost to my once again faltering ego and the extra money allowed me to keep my third floor apartment. The job allowed for full use of my creativity, leadership, and healing abilities. However, it was also extremely demanding, stressful, and exhausting. I neglected what was left of the commune even more and between all the changes in the group dynamic and the intense craziness, almost everyone involved had now come to a point of severe burnout. That winter all the remaining volunteers moved out of the house at 20th Street and other friends, none of whom wanted to be involved with *Magical Blend*, moved in. And so the *Magical Blend* commune passed out of history and into the realm of legends, leaving behind three great years of wonderful, mystical, and crazy fun.

I stayed in the apartment, using it both as my home and the office for the magazine, but things had certainly changed. By the end of that year, I was spending much more than 40 hours a week at Fred Finch, and much of my spare time with Deborah Genito. At the time, she was a social worker at Fred Finch, where we shared responsibility for the Tahoe House unit. Deborah was challenging then, and interestingly enough, still is—I expect that she always will be. In some ways, we have many of the same values, but in other ways we are nothing alike. She grew up in Connecticut and is second generation Italian. What a great cook and lover. She is a true healer. Her therapeutic work is amazing. The longer we worked together, the more deeply I fell in love with her. Yet she was resistant to anything New Age or metaphysical. Sometimes, even today, I think that Deborah likes spending time with me because she thinks that I'm seriously insane, and she has never met someone she believed was so crazy yet who functions so well in society. I brag about being crazy and wild and eccentric and hearing voices. Yet I know how to take care of what is important and where all the keys are kept. I realized soon after we met that I was falling in love with her. When I am with her I feel more complete, yet her very existence as an important player in my life constantly drives me even more to achieve my ambitions.

From the beginning, Deborah didn't like *Magical Blend*. She told me that it seemed to her to be a waste of my time and energies. I took that as another challenge to prove to her and the world that *Magical Blend* is an important publication. Always, it seemed, there were more dragons to slay and more spells to cast.

Magical Sales

Somehow, *Magical Blend* kept persevering through the dark nights. Mary Webster, a volunteer who worked days editing video magazines and Penny King, an amazing artist, pretty much put together issue #10 on their own. Jerry put many of the final *Magical Blend* touches into it, and our only ad salesman (since issue #7, when we began selling ads), Colyar Dupont, brought in enough money so that we could print it. It was slim and once again different and maybe lacked a bit of the old commune pizzazz, but it sold OK and the ball kept bouncing.

After the issue came out, Jerry and I called a volunteer meeting to plan for the future. No one came! The next night I called everyone. Everyone seemed burnt out and had made other commitments. Some made noises about wanting to get involved again in a few months. Others said they wanted to stay involved, just not every week. The times were certainly changing, and maybe not for the better, but Jerry and I refused to give in to our fears. We discussed the possibilities. We could call it quits and close it down or, as Jerry suggested, the two of us could just take as long as we needed to bring together the best issue possible, and worry about how to get it printed later.

Money kept trickling in slowly from distributors, bookstores, and subscribers, and Colyar agreed to sell ads once again for his usual commissions. We agreed that we could do it. If we put out the one we always wanted to do without any volunteers and it didn't do any better than the others, then we knew it would be time to stop. We would just quit and call it a rich experience. I knew I could do just fine working in human services, anyway, but still . . . I desperately wanted to keep the dream of *Magical Blend* alive. Like Caesar crossing the Rubicon, all we could do was take that decisive step, do our best, and then see what would happen.

My tenure at Fred Finch was a mixture of experiences. On the one hand, I had the honor to supervise some of the most wonderful, healing, and creative people I ever met. I loved them and will always treasure the times we shared. But they were also very worn out and stressed, so working with them proved to be quite demanding.

The program director and my boss, Curt Sugiyama, was a 50-year-old genius who grew up in the Japanese internment camps during the Second World War. Curt cared a great deal about fishing and was equally inspired when it came to operating organizations. I learned very much from him and he expected a great deal from me in return. Another close friend that I met at Fred Finch was Roger Spence. He was a very dedicated chaplain and assistant activities director/social worker. I had never before met such an open-minded Hindu/Buddhist-like Christian.

Jerry and I worked on issue #11 throughout the latter portion of 1984. Finally, shortly after the New Year, we delivered it to the printer. We made it the best issue we could, with an eye towards sales. After almost five years and ten issues, we believed that we knew what the readers wanted. I missed most of the volunteers but it was refreshing to have just Jerry and me putting the magazine together and Colyar selling ads. We had art by Jeff Fletcher, an article and comics by Steven Spears, a piece from Van Ault, and two more by Anne Hiddenone and Ed Ellsworth. So the volunteers were still well represented, just edited and framed in a new and improved fashion. And of course, Silma Smith, dependable Silma Smith, who had proofread so many issues for us in the past, did this one out of her love and dedication one more time.

In April of 1985, Deborah moved in with me at the 20th Street apartment. The two of us occupied the whole third floor, but I kept the largest room for *Magical Blend*'s office. Issue #11 had been on sale for several weeks at that point, and Jerry and I were anxiously waiting for information about how it would sell. Then, slowly, we began to hear back from the bookstores and distributors. Many wanted to reorder; most asked to increase their order for upcoming issues. When the dust settled, it was clear that issue #11 had sold out practically everywhere we had put it, as never before, in record time! Jerry and I had succeeded! We had finally figured out what our potential readers wanted.

The first week of May, a new director by the name of Ms. King took over at Fred Finch. She immediately took a liking to the residential psychiatrist and a dislike to me and my mentor, program director Curt Sugiyama. She called me into her office. "I have heard of your antics here at Fred Finch," she said. "I want you to know that my goal is to make this a hospital, not a resort. Your renegade Tahoe House will either get with the program and operate as an institution should or you will no longer have a job." I looked out her corner window over at my beloved Tahoe House. My friends and co-workers Lillian, Kerrie, and Paul were sitting out front on the couch, talking with some of the kids. I felt terrible as I realized that my dream of unconditional love and healing was coming to a close. I looked at the wind blowing in the sycamore tree in front of the house and the green grass in the quadrant between the office building and the four houses. My sadness was powerful and immediate.

I barely held back my tears. "No, I can't even attempt to do what you ask," I said. "I think it would be better if I didn't help you bring about what you want to do." I was crying uncontrollably as I walked over to Tahoe House, where I informed the staff and kids that I had resigned. Then I cleaned out my desk and left.

The first thing I did when I got home was to call Jerry and tell him that I now planned to work full time as the publisher of *Magical Blend.* Then I went to bed. It seems I slept for most of the next two weeks. Deborah had decided to stay at Fred Finch for another six months and check it out, so I'd get up in the mornings and see her off to work. Then I would return to bed. I would get up and file some papers and make a few phone calls. Then back to bed.

Around that time, Jerry decided that he had worked too long at his job. His company was in dire financial trouble and was holding everyone's paycheck. Jerry resigned his real world job and then joined in an employee lawsuit against the owner. He also started showing up for work at my apartment at 9 A.M. every morning. This put an end to my habit of sleeping in, but it was great motivation to get me up and moving on the magazine. Issue #11 had not only sold out but had also garnered massive subscription sales. We were hopeful that after five years and ten issues with volunteers, we had set the stage for *Magical Blend* to become a real magazine and a real business, with paid employees and everything. Yet we were both scared. Could we run the company day-to-day? How would it be done? Would there be enough money to at least pay ourselves minimum wage while publishing a magazine that would change and improve the world? Could we possibly accomplish both, or were we just dreaming?

That year and the five that followed were a transition from a crazy anarchistic volunteer group who got together on occasions to produce magazines, to a creative and yet efficient business which had loving limits and rules and encouraged creativity but was no longer pure chaos. We hired about a third of the volunteers who were involved up until issue #9. The others remained friends, confidants, and advisors.

Between issues #11 and #12, Colyar received a large family inheritance and sadly resigned his position as advertising sales manager. Jerry and I decided to take over in his place, even though neither of us had ever sold much advertising up until that time. We immediately did a mailing to 500 potential advertisers, explaining our business and why they should advertise with us, and included a simple media kit with a copy of issue #11, ad prices, and demographics. It was our second full week when this project was completed. In that time, we had set up all new systems and had put out a large mailing. Subscription orders, wholesale revenues, and retail sales were all up. We were optimistic.

When Deborah got home that night, she invited Jerry to stay for supper. We ate, drank wine, and celebrated our new career. We were so excited and proud of our potential that we drank lots more wine than maybe we should have. At about midnight, we called Jerry a cab. When he was going down the stairs he tripped. I called down to him, asking if he was OK. He said that he was, but when he got into the taxi, he was bleeding like a gutted fish. The driver took him to the emergency ward instead of home. He ended up with ten stitches. When he finally got home, his lover Bill was not happy about our impromptu celebration. To make it up to him, we had Bill and Jerry over to eat a few months later. Bill was a nice man, but he was extremely worried about his health. Many people that Bill and Jerry knew had died of AIDS, and Bill was very fearful of that terrible disease.

Earlier that year, before we knew that issue #11 would be such a breakthrough, I had made a deal with Jeff Fletcher and his friend and apartment mate, Matthew Courtway. Matthew was a tall, redheaded, very sweet man. He was a poet and an artist who did weird spray paint murals that many people just adored. He loved *Magical Blend* but felt that it needed to radically alter its direction. The deal was that Jeff and Matthew could make the majority of the editorial and design choices on #12 if they came up with half the printing costs. Jeff had always been very generous and financially helpful throughout our first five years. So in some ways this seemed to me in my desperation to be a logical next step. As #12 came together, it was clear that it would be very different from anything that had come before. We lucked out when Penny King got to know and interview the actor-comedian, Robin Williams. It was nice to meet him; he seemed very genuine and real. The interview came out great, and Jeff and Matthew agreed to include it in #12.

It turned out that Jerry and I were terrible ad sales people. Our mailing brought in not one sale. We had neither the training nor the experience needed to succeed. When someone said no to buying an ad, it felt as though they were saying that *Magical Blend* was invalid, and so was I. We needed to generate at least $10,000 to pay us minimum wage for eight weeks, cover half the printing costs, and mail the copies to subscribers, bookstores, and distributors. Jerry and I both began rewriting our resumes and considering our options.

In August, just when it appeared that we would never get our act together, Curt Sugiyama volunteered to become *Magical Blend*'s consultant—for free! Curt had also left Fred Finch by that time. He was seeing clients in therapy and doing custom cabinet design, so he was doing OK in terms of income. Like me, he gets bored easily and we had developed a great friendship, so he became my weekly business advisor. I would drive to his home in Marin, where he went over our cash flow and spreadsheets. Consultants like that are worth their weight in gold, yet Curt did it at no cost. He really helped me get a firm handle on the business side of things. Yet even with Curt's guidance and support, Jerry and I continued to have little success selling ads for issue #12. We had spent most of the money that issues #10 and #11 had made and brought very little back. Clearly, we needed to do something to increase our advertising revenue.

Ed Ellsworth, who was a protégé of John Lilly and had written our whale and dolphin column for years, had started a successful computer systems sales business. Ed had a paranoid and schizophrenic salesman by the name of Charles Leagues whom he had to get rid of smoothly. Ed called me up and begged me to take Charles off his hands.

Charles and I spoke and reached an arrangement: He would sell ads for #12 on commission only, working on my back porch and living in his van. Charles was intense and very difficult to supervise but he could sell. When we finally got issue #12 all laid out and pasted up, we still needed quite a bit of money to pay for printing. We were very worried until Charles made a contact with Ramana Das and Uma Silbey, the Marin-based couple who played wonderful New Age music, wrote, and created fantastic works of jewelry. Charles convinced them to advertise their jewelry in a five-page insert at the beginning of the issue. They paid us much more than we needed for printing. As a result, Charles got a healthy commission and Jerry and I got to pay ourselves, our past due bills, and the printer.

Charles was more difficult to supervise than anyone I had supervised up to that point, but his last-minute deal made everything right financially. So we agreed to continue with our arrangement. I just hoped that he could keep selling, and maybe even get an apartment and move out of his car. At least I didn't have to apply for a day job just yet.

It was funny that Ramana Das and Uma Silbey were the ones who saved us on issue #12, because our path and theirs had crossed before. In the early years of the magazine, during a time after Maria and before Deborah when I was unattached, Ramana Das had invited everyone on the staff to a Saturday night party at their home in Marin. I went over with Steven Spears, Jeff Fletcher, and a few of the other volunteers. We had a great time to say the least. Ramana Das and Uma had a very lovely house with a hot tub, and a number of gorgeous young women who worked for them. Steven, Jeff, and I couldn't believe our luck—it was like every young man's fantasy come true. Beautiful and friendly women, ecstasy and cocaine, fine wine and a hot tub—ahhh, nights like that come so seldom but leave such memories. Isn't that how life is supposed to be? Why do any of us settle for less rather than live in a state constant, joyous ecstasy? More to the point, how does a reformed Catholic boy from New England write of the tantric details of that party? Perhaps I should just leave it to your imagination. All I will say is that Ramana Das and Uma, though since separated as a couple, will for more than one reason always have my deepest gratitude for all they added to my life.

Charles indirectly caused us to establish the first *Magical Blend* office that didn't double as someone's home. Deborah found Charles to be extremely creepy and couldn't stand having him work in the apartment. She loved having me and Jerry around all the time, but started saying that either Charles and the magazine went or she was going to have to move out. William Stewart, still a good friend, had a small, windowless office space south of Market on Bryant Street that he was willing to sublet to us for a very affordable monthly rent. It was about four and a half desks long and about two desks wide, with just barely enough room for chairs. Charles called it the Jesse James gang hideout. I was never sure which of us was supposed to be Jesse James and I didn't want to ask. However, by renting this office, I was able to keep my love life alive, and those volunteers who were still interested could work nights.

The first thing Charles did when we moved into the new office was to cover the wall in front of his desk with pictures of himself and Christ. I always suspected that he thought he was the reincarnation of Christ, or at least the personification of the second coming or something exalted like that. But he sold ads and made us money, so I figured I wouldn't ask his thoughts about his connection to Jesus. Even with Charles's efforts, however, at that time we brought in a much greater amount of cash from subscriptions, distributors, and bookstores than from advertising. I knew that with most other magazines, this situation was reversed, but at that time, we hadn't cracked the advertising market as I had hoped and prayed that we would. Plus, people couldn't find New Age, mystical information such as we were printing anywhere else. So subscriptions and newsstand sales kept growing and bringing in better and better income, while advertising continued to straggle along.

Around that time, I got a new pair of roommates. Gloria did tortured sexual Jesus art and Peter was the singer and lead guitarist for a popular punk rock band, The Toiling Midgets (also known as The Working Little People). They had a record out and it was selling well. Both Gloria and Peter were brilliant people, college educated, and uniquely insightful. When Peter lost his job and they couldn't pay the rent, I gave him a job at *Magical Blend* opening bookstores. He would call independent stores from coast to coast and ask them if they carried magazines. If they did or were interested in doing so, he'd tell them all about *Magical Blend* and either sign them up or send out a copy and follow up in a week. He got $5 for every store he opened. Peter was a natural—so charming and brilliant. Gloria and Peter stayed current with their rent and opened more bookstores than we ever had before. He didn't stay on staff for very long, and the experiment of them as roommates ended quickly as well. They were a side note worth mentioning, though.

Curt Sugiyama and I continued our invaluable weekly meetings. In addition to his wise instruction on developing spreadsheets, budgets, and cash flow projections, we would discuss at length how to split responsibilities between Jerry and me, how to supervise Charles, and how to add staff wisely. My sister Pat had lost her job as the secretary/bookkeeper at Borrmann Steel Co., where she had been for a while. So we hired her to be our office manager. A new guy, Andy Willis, came to us as well. He loved *Magical Blend* and wanted to work with us. He seemed brilliant but a bit emotionally unsettled. He was very good at selling ads and expanding our distribution in imaginative ways. Steven Spears and Van Ault came by regularly to work with some new volunteers a few nights a week. Jeff Fletcher and Matthew Courtway were both working in a phone sales room for the Shriners until Christmas, after which time they planned to began selling ads for us full time. It seemed surreal to me, but we were developing into a real business, even though none of us were sure what that meant.

As we tried to figure out ways to deal with the radical changes occurring with the business and in our lives, we naturally turned to magic. I remember some spells for success that we used in those days that still work well today:

1. Get a room full of people who are open to magic being real and who want your business to succeed. Agree on three to five important goals for the next six months. Then light a candle

and some incense. Call on the spiritual essences of your business. Call on whatever other spiritual powers will listen and take effect. Tell them your goals. Pray for their assistance. Chant together. Pitch one goal at a time. Then, going around in the circle, let each person speak as many details as they can imagine about what it will be like when this goal is achieved. At the end, extinguish the candle and incense and recite, "So Mote It Be!"

2. Sage has been used from time immemorial to clear out old stuck energies. It is a simple tool you can buy at most health food stores. In many businesses, people who used to work there leave their energies and even attitudes and interests behind, usually unconsciously. This affects the work environment. As the boss, I often stay late and do a cleansing ritual in which I light some sage and walk about the office with it burning in an abalone shell. I pray aloud, saying, "Old energies, old employees, your time here is over. Please go to where you can do more good. Please leave this office and return no more."

3. A companion process to energy clearing is calling in and installing positive energies. I have done this ritual with staff and on my own. The best time is at night or on the weekend when the office is quiet and no one is working. Lighting a white or red candle will help focus the energies—the white for new beginnings, or the red for keeping most of what is in place but bringing more enthusiasm, inspiration, or passion into the workplace. Walk about the office with the candle, praying that these energies fill every crack and crevice. See in your mind's eye the energies you are calling having a positive effect on everyone who works there.

4. Grounding is done to keep the energies of a business connected to the Earth and receiving Mother Nature's blessings on

what you are doing. See in your mind cords connecting the corners of your business space, tying in the center, and going down deep into the Earth. See all negative situations and energies going down this cord and see healing, growth energy coming up and assisting in your business goals.

5. If you are experiencing challenges with an individual employee or co-worker, sit in their chair and talk to them when they are not there. Paint rainbows everywhere around the workspace in your imagination. Ask angels for help.

Printers

In those early years, the printers were as interesting and challenging as the celebrities or the staff. Every printer we worked with seemed to be an intense character. The first three issues were printed in Sacramento. Issue #4 was printed in Kansas City, Missouri, because we got a great price and cheaper shipping to the East Coast. But after one issue, those people realized that we weren't exactly normal Christians and wouldn't print us any more. As a consequence, issue #5 was shipped to South Carolina for the color-printing break. It turned out that they too were devout, close-minded Christians. They insisted on turning any picture that had any sexual element, even fetuses, upside down or side ways on the page. The ones that we didn't catch on the printer's proofs were printed that way in the magazine when it finally came out. I say "finally" because just as the issue was being printed that winter, the entire state of South Carolina got socked with a huge, freak snowstorm. They closed everything for two weeks, so the plant became backed up with printing jobs. Since we weren't Christian, they held our job for five weeks. When they delivered it, we paid only a quarter of the agreed-upon price, so I suppose everything worked out for the best.

We sent issue #6 to a new printer in Michigan. It was to have a color cover but black and white inside. Our agreement was to pay half when we sent the boards and the other half sixty days later. At that point, we owed four printers for portions of their remaining bills. I found a new printer in San Francisco who agreed to print issue #7 very inexpensively and only wanted a third down to begin. We delivered the issue to them and then checked the presses every day. The printing quality was good but the scheduling was sporadic. I took to driving to the printing company most days, waiting for them to get going, and then making sure that they were working on our magazine properly. I think that the owner had a drug problem and his press operator had a drinking problem. When the issue was finally printed, the owner called me to explain that his collating machine was broken beyond repair. He made us an offer. If we could rally 25 people and have them staple the magazines together by hand and place them in the boxes, he would reduce our price by 1/3 and we wouldn't have to pay the rest until we were able.

People we had! A *Magical Blend* coalition meeting was called and friends came out of the woodwork to help. We had the issue collated and boxed in no time. We even had a deal worked out for issue #8. But as soon as we paid him for issue #7, he informed us that he was going out of business. We offered to buy the printing company on a payment plan, but he wanted cash and we were cash poor.

Issue #8 was printed by a local printer in Oakland. For issue #9, I got a great bid from a printing company in Los Angeles, so I flew down with the boards and original art in an artist portfolio carrying case. Now in those days, you used to cut the type and wax it onto layout boards. Then you would wax on little word or sentence patches over the typesetting errors. The plane got hot, the wax melted, and I arrived in L.A. with a mess. I did my best to rewax the corrections but it was tricky figuring out what went where. When I reread issue #9 today, the errors I made are still painfully obvious.

Little by little we paid off the old printers. Beginning with issue #10, we began printing the magazine at a little print shop in

San Jose. By now, I had an old Chevy van, which we would use to drive the boards down as well as stop by for printer proof and press checks. I would actually sleep in the van, so that as the printing was being done and the plates were being changed, even if it was in the middle of the night, I would be right there to approve the color matches and the degree of black ink being laid down. However, that printer too went bankrupt right after we paid him off for issue #13.

The Benefits of Perseverance

I have a burning drive inside of me that believes in *Magical Blend* magazine and MB Media. I believe they have made positive contributions to the world for decades. Countless people have thanked me for the inspiration and sense of community that *Magical Blend* has given them. I don't think that I could ever completely walk away from this magazine, or allow it to become something it was never meant to be. Sometimes I wish I could curse and bless every human on the planet with a similar devotion to a creative project that they truly believe in. I love my life and feel extremely blessed in countless ways. I go to sleep nights exhausted and looking forward to the next stage in MB Media's evolution.

I know from the cards, letters, e-mails, and phone calls that we have succeeded in touching many lives and inspiring countless people. I believe we have provided community for the isolated and encouragement for the discouraged. I believe that *Magical Blend* has made a great contribution to the world and humanity and has assisted in planting seeds that will eventually bring about a Golden Age on the planet.

But the great thing is that anyone reading these words can do the same thing. I urge everyone who is willing to risk and believe in their own vision to do as we have done. Just make simple plans, do some research, put away a little spare cash if you can, and begin to create the project of your dreams. Always be willing to adapt, remain flexible and resourceful, but know that you can do it. As

Jimmy Cliff sang, "You must try, try, and try, try, and try. You'll succeed at last!" You won't always know nor be guided clearly as to what to do next or what will happen next year. However, plan the best you can, prepare for the worst, but expect and work for the best. Work with your havingness issues, face the personal lies and deep subconscious beliefs that you accepted from childhood, and then work to transmute them all to high joy, creativity, prosperity, and a spiritual life.

Business-wise, these years tested both *Magical Blend* and me. If it were easy, everyone would do it. As it is, many people and companies launch magazines, yet only the very dedicated succeed. We had a vision. We had a dream. The volunteers came and went, sometimes all at once. We could have thrown in the towel at many points. Instead, we kept telling ourselves that the darkest hour is usually the moment just before the dawn. We gave it all we had time and time again. For example, we made issue #11 everything we thought *Magical Blend* could be, just when we needed it most. I'm sure that we would have committed to do it again and again, even if issue #11 had failed.

In business as in life, it is important to be willing to persevere and to risk everything. If you give up because it didn't work out as you thought it would, or because you failed on your first attempt, then you will never know success. If you see every setback, failure, surprise, and difficulty as an opportunity to adapt and create a better way, a better system, a better magazine, a better magical spell, or a better life, then the only limitation you will experience will be in your imagination. I have failed often. I have made more embarrassing mistakes than I care to think about. I have smelly feet when I take my boots off at night. I am not my successes. I am not my failures. These things just happen to me! I am me. I like myself and believe in my dreams, goals, and visions, and I am dedicated to doing whatever I can to turn them into reality. *Magical Blend* magazine is not its worst issue; it is not its best issue. It is an essence that through good business is changing and healing the world. Everyone can begin at any moment they decide to create such a business, to change the world, and to live out their dream. All that is required is determination, adaptability, creativity, and a willingness to make the most of what you have, as well as a sense of humor and the ability to laugh at yourself. But it certainly doesn't hurt to get a good business advisor like Curt Sugiyama!

FOUR

MAKING A BUSINESS—ISSUES 13–15 (1986)

A Real Office

As 1986 began, we found ourselves in our first real office, on Bryant Street in the South of Market neighborhood. In addition to six paid staff members, we had maintained our far-flung group of volunteers. My sister Pat turned out to be a great office manager, and my new friend Richard Daab came aboard as a writer/special projects editor. It was awfully tight when all of us were in the tiny office, but the coziness did make it easier for us to work together.

One of my personal highlights of that time was when I got to speak with Yoko Ono. I found her to be rather distant, guarded, and business-like, but she permitted us to print an interview someone else did with her. It appeared in issue #15, which came out later that year. It was incredible to imagine the kind of life she had and everything that she had seen. So rich! So famous! What did she know about John's death? Did the CIA have her blackmailed? What a rush.

Around that time, Jerry's aunt died and left him a substantial inheritance, a portion of which he used to purchase a newly released Macintosh computer with a laser writer printer. Not many people or businesses owned desktop computers in 1986. We were now able to do all of our typesetting on computer. The little DOS-based computers we had been using up until then were very impressive but difficult to use. Jerry knew basic computer programming and could fix any problem any of us had in a flash. However, whenever he wasn't there I would get so frustrated that I just wanted to throw the computers out the one office window we had. With our new setup, I no longer had to drive down to Oakland to bring the printer the typewritten editorial, go back to pick it up, go back down to bring the corrections, and then go back to pick those up. We didn't even have to wax on the boards or corrections anymore. I have had a love-hate relationship with technology for most of my life, but that experience definitely leaned toward love. I especially love Apple computers—what a great company! What a huge step forward for us!

Issue #13, which had come out right at the beginning of the year, sold out of its 15,000 copy print order in record time. That was really one great issue. We had a wonderful article from Joan Ocean, who had a great book out at the time named *Dolphin Tears and Dreams*. She meditated with dolphins and they told her the most beautiful things. The cover featured a dolphin painting by Jean-Luc Bozzoli. Now this man was cool. He grew up in France and had never painted, but one day just decided he should become a painter. He had a friend take him to a deserted island in the Pacific with enough food for six months. He stayed there alone and taught himself to paint. The dolphins would come to the beach and he would paint gorgeous pictures of them. Now that is a very original story.

Things continued to get better and better for *Magical Blend* as the year went on. We made contact with Carlos Castaneda for the first time, getting an exclusive interview as well as his permission to run it. What an intense, mysterious, and otherworldly fellow he was. We printed the first half of the interview in issue #14 and the second half in issue #15. That interview really brought *Magical Blend* national attention. We were hot as spiritual trends go. *Magical Blend* went from obscurity to renown in many circles and those issues sure didn't hurt.

We began to find ourselves solicited by many famous and semifamous people who wanted us to interview them. One of these folks was the "Godfather of Crystal Awareness," Marcel Vogel. He had been a high-level engineer at IBM who had taken early retirement. IBM held his contributions to their company in such high regard that they gave him a micron telescope as a goodbye present. With this powerful instrument and his unique genius, insights, and scientific skills, Marcel and his wife set about studying and growing healing crystals. They were a major force behind the dawning mainstream awareness of crystals as effective spiritual tools and *Magical Blend* spotlighted their work, in addition to that being done by Dale Walker, Uma Silbey, and other amazing and important crystal experts.

I interviewed Christopher Hyatt, a man who claimed to be the only true head of the only true Golden Dawn. Well, there have been many others who have made that same claim. Hyatt was intelligent and insightful—maybe he is the real one? The legacy of Alistair Crowley and his contemporary Golden Dawn founders is well fought over. Yet all of these folks seem to get lost in the traditions, rituals, and ceremonies, and lose sight of the importance of effective magic and joy that people can use in their lives. Crowley at least had a great sense of humor. I have read and gained much from many Golden Dawn-related books but I would warn people against joining any Golden Dawn cult.

During this time, I also met Anton LaVey, who wrote *The*

Satanic Bible. He introduced himself to us and offered to write articles just for *Magical Blend*. I refused. I had read his book and found it to be evil! It encouraged people to do the opposite of what *Magical Blend* stands for. This book was all about hurting people and exploiting them for selfish gains and sadistic enjoyment. It stated that the only hope for happiness is egotistical self-fulfillment, for the world is bad and the only way to succeed in it is to be bad as well. I was clear that this man was never writing for us! One of *Magical Blend*'s editorial and advertising rules has always been that nothing can be of the dark side. Any material that speaks of causing harm or getting revenge or exploiting others has never had a place in *Magical Blend*, and never will.

Taxes the Wild Way (Do Not Try This at Home!)

That spring we had to do payroll taxes for the first time. What a daunting and complicated undertaking! I spent days learning the formulas and calculating the appropriate deduction for everyone we had on staff. Up until that time, we had been paying everyone as subcontractors of a sort, but now we were all in one office and working 40 hours a week. I gave everyone their first paycheck, sent the government agencies their cuts with accompanying paperwork, and hoped for the best.

It didn't take long for me to receive a very official-looking letter from the IRS. They notified me that everything had been calculated and deducted incorrectly. I was advised to hire an accounting service to do it right. So we hired an inexpensive person who said he could come in once a week and do it. The government reporting agencies didn't agree with his figures either. So we hired a professional payroll service.

Now, when a similar experience began to unfold with Jerry's and my state and federal tax returns, you would think I would have learned, but not me. Fortunately (we thought) Charles had a friend who would redo our taxes at a reasonable price. Even better, we didn't have to pay until the work was finished.

We gave Charles's friend all of the receipts along with the income statements and expense books. A month later, we still hadn't heard from this young lady, so we began hounding her. She eventually called us with the good news that our taxes were done and that we could come get the returns. When we arrived at her apartment, we found her six-foot, two-inch hulk of a boyfriend waiting for us. He said pay first or no taxes. We did. She gave us back our records along with the tax forms. We could tell from just a glance that they were done incorrectly. When we began to complain, her boyfriend said, "Look, we deal cocaine from here and we have many mean friends who owe us favors. Take what you got and forget it if you want to stay in one piece." It sounded like good advice, so we took our once again botched returns and went to a regular accountant. I should have known better than to take the advice of Charles Leagues on something like that.

This story shows how my responsibilities had changed by that time. As publisher, my role was that of supervisor, organizer, planner, and communicator. Everyone's opinions were still considered, but as time went by, Jerry and I became more comfortable in meeting daily to make all of the major decisions. I look back to that time and remember that it used to take me up to a week to craft my 1,000 word "Potentials" column, which I always viewed as the doorway inviting our readers into each issue. I always wanted it to say to the reader: "Yes, our art might be far out and somewhat scary, and the editorial may be esoteric, occult, and intellectual, but *Magical Blend* is really about the important things that you can use every day in your life. Come on in for a swim—once you get use to it, the water's fine and the experience will stretch your brain and improve your existence!"

Sometimes, after a week of agonizing, that message would shine through. But now I think of taking a week to write 1,000 words and I laugh. Back then, I'd usually arrive at the office around seven or eight in the morning. I was often the first one there, provided that no one had pulled an all-nighter or had come in early because they couldn't sleep. My days would alternate between planning, working on wise growth, troubleshooting, and fire fighting. Jerry and I would discuss editorial decisions at length. I would meet with staff to review what they were doing and how they were going about it. It seemed we were always placing ads and interviewing applicants for new positions. Whenever staff was sick I would attempt to make sure their responsibilities were covered.

There weren't any restaurants in the neighborhood around our first office, so I seldom ate lunch. However, once we moved to the Golden Gate Theater building, there were tons of restaurants so I would usually take an hour-long break to enjoy lunch.

Everything about our business represented a steep learning curve for me. I had to figure out how to manage cash flow and do spread sheets, payroll, payroll taxes, and annual federal taxes. On the personnel side, I needed to learn how to hire, train, supervise, manage, and sometimes fire people. I don't think I ever fully mastered any of these skills; however, I spent lots of important time studying and working on these elements of our business back then. When we were late for deadlines or had an important project that I could make a difference on, I would stay as late as I was productive, which sometimes lasted all night. However, with Deborah waiting at home and money seeming good, I usually left between 5:30 and 6 P.M.

Adventures and Misadventures

After much fruitless searching, we finally found a reasonably priced printer for issue #14. We called him the Lobsterman. He was old as dirt, had bad arthritis, and spoke in such a gravelly voice that you could barely understand him. He and his son, Junior, did almost all the work at their plant, with the help of a few part-time assistants. They promised us tons of extras on the printing, but once we gave them their large down payment and the work began, they denied having promised us anything. In fact, they then began demanding higher and higher cost adjustments to the original bid. This man was so cheap that he had bought his own ancient garbage truck to crush and recycle his paper trimmings.

When the issue was done, Lobsterman refused to print the subscriber cards and envelopes, or even to give us magazines, until we paid the second half of the bill and an extra $6,000 they had added in as unforeseen costs. This presented quite a dilemma— we were doing well, but we didn't have anywhere near that amount of money on hand, and the subscribers, distributors, and bookstores were waiting for the new issue. Plus it was unfair business practice! However, he wouldn't give an inch nor let us have even one advance copy.

Fortunately, Junior wasn't too bright. He liked us and seemed to resent his dad. So, with some undercover detective work, we figured out what times Lobsterman usually left Junior alone at the plant. We pulled up in my van at the appropriate time and acted surprised that Lobsterman was gone. We gave Junior a small check and told him that his dad had said that we could pay the rest later. He helped us load up my van with 10,000 copies of the magazine. A short time later, we returned for the remainder of the copies as well as all of our original artwork. We did send Lobsterman an additional $3,000 eventually when he agreed not to sue us. We had to print the subscription cards and envelopes at a local letter shop, open every box and stuff them into every magazine before we shipped them all out.

In my book, there are good printers and bad printers, trustworthy printers and devious printers. In those days, we were always on the lookout for printers that could offer high quality, reasonable prices, fast turnaround, and good payment plans. That tended to place us with some sweet-talking but rather shady and inept printers. I am glad to report that things have improved greatly in recent years.

Issue #14 was the last one we delivered to the San Francisco Bay Area retailers ourselves. It had gotten so I would spend a whole week out of the office after an issue was printed, driving to every city on the map from Santa Rosa to Santa Cruz. The revenues were good but that is what magazine distributors are supposed to do, not publishers! It became increasingly obvious that I could make us more money by staying in the office than by delivering magazines to bookstores, so I gave up my magazine delivery route and concentrated on growing our business.

Famous Folks

Everyone in the office was very excited when Terence McKenna agreed to appear in issue #15. He was introduced to me by Faustin Bray. Faustin owns Sound Photosynthesis, a company that records lectures from cutting-edge thinkers and then sells the videos and audio tapes. Faustin had known John Lilly and Tim Leary since the 1960s. She knows virtually everyone who is anyone on the fringe. Nowadays, she does a regular radio program on KPFA in Berkley, on which she interviews all the movers and shakers. At that time, Terence was just starting to make a name and reputation for himself on the international New Age stage. He was, however, already a legendary figure in San Francisco. His first two books were uniquely insightful, and I was quite impressed with him and his way of viewing the world. He was a bit like Robert Anton Wilson and Tim Leary in that he could think so fast and make connections that most people would never see.

Terence was known for his expertise on hallucinogens, especially psilocybin mushrooms and DMT. Yet his books should be required reading for every high school student. He was just that brilliant. He was a bit overly proud of his extended vocabulary, perhaps, but extremely personable nonetheless. How I enjoyed the lively conversations that we shared. Terence's view of history was that it truly revolved around illicit imports such as sugar, coffee, opium, tobacco, rum, marijuana, LSD, and cocaine. He believed that politics, war, and economics have less to do with principles and more to do with the fact that these activities are all covers for smuggling and the widespread use of illegal substances. He also believed that time and history are drawing humanity and the Earth to a horizon line where time and space will cease to exist and will be replaced by the realm of imagination. It was his conviction that at some time after the year 2012, telepathy and the ability to create whatever we can imagine will be available to humans. All events previous to this were only setting the stage for this age. I am hardly doing justice to his perspectives in this very abbreviated recap, but suffice it to say that in many ways, Terence was the most eloquent and purely intellectual person I had ever met. Tim Leary, John Lilly, and Robert Anton Wilson all pioneered a movement that involved drugs, and all spoke about people looking at their own selves and figuring out how to develop personal insights instead of buying into a bunch of propaganda. Terence McKenna continued this tradition, and it was our great privilege to feature him in our pages on several occasions.

Magical Blend by this time had established a reputation as a place people could turn to for information on all manner of mystical experiences and events. One experience I remember clearly from those days was the time when Antro Allie invited me to meet author José Argeülles. I greatly enjoyed his book *The Mayan Factor,* and he was just beginning to coordinate an international event called the Harmonic Convergence. José claimed that if enough people got together and meditated or prayed or did ritual on this astrologically auspicious day, then we would have a unique opportunity to jump-start humanity's future. José had come by this information while studying the ancient Mayans and their calendar. He claimed that the Gregorian calendar was a mistake, and that it and timepieces took humanity away from nature's rhythms. He believed that if we returned to the 13-moon Mayan calendar and gave up our clocks and watches, then humanity would begin living the Golden Age almost at once. Antro agreed to interview him in order to give his Harmonic Convergence a boost. Not surprisingly, José was having difficulty getting the word out on his rather radical theories. After we featured him in an interview, the Harmonic Convergence took off and was mentioned everywhere from Doonesbury cartoons to *Newsweek*.

Thanks in no small part to the interviews with Carlos Castaneda and Marcel Vogel, issue #14 was the second issue of *Magical Blend* to sell out immediately. We were so pleased that we offered them both a column. True to his image, Carlos turned us down, but Marcel accepted, provided that Jerry and I would drive to his office before every issue and do his column in an interview format. We agreed. Jerry was a wonderful editor who was terrific at taking raw material and making it into fantastic editorial content. I wish that Carlos had accepted. However, due to the hunger in the public for this information and his unwillingness to attempt to fill that need, we felt that we had to begin searching for other naguals and shamans that could pick up where he left off.

We have been fortunate in that creative and well-known folks were always interested in what we were doing. Early on, when we all still worked and mostly lived in the 20th Street commune, we invited a famous artist to dinner who had been featured in our pages. The artist said that he would be there with his girlfriend, who also happened to be an artist of some renown. The staff got excited and prepared a great dinner. The artist didn't call or come. We waited forever and then called his number—no answer. We eventually ate and drank. About midnight, we were all done and rather drunk when the doorbell rang. It was the two famous artists, and they too were drunk. They said that they hoped they weren't too late but they had been inspired to cocreate a painting and it couldn't wait. They hadn't eaten, though, and were starving. We told them we had kept their dinner warm. We sat them down and poured them some wine while someone went to get their plates out of the oven. It was placed in front of them and unveiled with great pomp and ceremony. However, someone had left the oven on high and the meal we had saved for them was burned black and unrecognizable—definitely inedible. They were confused as were the rest of us. Being a bachelor at the time, there was little food at my house. I ended up making them peanut butter and jelly sandwiches to have with their wine. We all laughed for hours. I am told that the artist still tells that story today.

Over the years, I have had the opportunity to speak with some amazingly influential people, but it was sometimes a shock to find out they are not always the images they project to the public. For instance, I met one of the most well-known spiritual authors of the time, someone who had been on TV a great deal. I asked him if we could use a talk he had just given as an article for *Magical Blend*. His gratifying reply was, "Yes, of course! I respect your magazine a great deal. It's about time I appeared in it!" After the article came out, he sent us a letter thanking us and saying how much he enjoyed the issue, about which we were very pleased.

A year or so later, I arranged to interview him through his agent to follow up on what I thought was our growing relationship. But when I got to speak with him on the phone, I barely recognized his voice. He was in a foul mood. He asked what magazine I was with, and, when I told him, he said I should send him one because he didn't think he had ever seen it. I attempted to remind him of our previous exchange, but he seemed dismissive. As we progressed with the interview, everything he said was extremely pessimistic. He responded to every question with an answer about how weak and lazy and untrustworthy humans are. He expressed little hope for the planet's future. I became more and more disheartened, trying desperately to get him to say something positive that I could use.

He had told me at the beginning that I could have twenty minutes of his time. After we had used exactly nineteen of those minutes, he said, "Well, that should do it. I have to go now." When I got off the phone, I was crushed and disappointed. How could one of the pillars of New Age spirituality be so grouchy? How could he express such pessimistic views? I wasn't sure what I should do about it, and agonized over whether I should let the world know the "other side" of this person. What was my editorial responsibility? Was there anything to be gained from letting people know "the truth"? How would it serve the magazine's purpose if we disillusioned our readers about this man the way I had been disillusioned? Most of all, was there anything in the interview at all that I could salvage?

In the end, I decided that there was not. I told the staff that he must have been having an "off" day and that we should just quote his book instead of using what I taped. We chose an appropriately upbeat and insightful excerpt from the book and went with that instead. Comparing the interview with the excerpt, it was like they came from two different people.

A few months later, I arranged for one of our editors to re-interview him. I guess I just wanted to give him another chance. To my delight, on this day he was "on." He remembered *Magical Blend* and greeted the editor warmly. He quoted his own books as answers to the questions. He was very optimistic and his view of the future was rosy. He was inspiring and enlightening.

I was once again reminded that even the greatest spiritual teachers are human. No one is optimistic all the time; everyone has "off" days. Enlightenment isn't a permanent condition; even the best of us have to work at it every day. And I also learned that, when dealing with famous people, sometimes it's best just to "pay no attention to the man behind the curtain."

Then there was the time when I had an extremely bizarre Monday morning conversation with a famous author. It was around 9 A.M., and I was just getting going at the office when one of the staff said that I had a phone call. It was from this well-known author, whom I had been trying to persuade to write for *Magical Blend,* or at least give us an interview, with little success. Thus, this out-of-the-blue phone call was a pleasant surprise. When I got on the phone, the surprises continued. The conversation proceeded as follows:

W: Michael, how are you? How is your family? How is your farm? How is the magazine doing?

M: Fine, fine, fine, and fine, and how are you?

W: Well, that is why I called. Michael, I need some favors from you.

M: Sure, anything for you.

W: Yes, that is what she told me you would say.

M: She?

W: Yes, you must promise never to tell anyone what I am going to tell you. Unless someday I say you can.

M: OK.

W: You're Jewish, aren't you?

M: Well, no. Many people seem to assume that, but I'm not. I am a bit of every religion but mostly pagan or pantheist.

W: But you were raised Jewish, though, weren't you?

M: No, I was around the Jewish faith a great deal growing up, but in truth, I was raised Catholic.

W: Oh, that's why she picked you. That's why she said you were one of hers.

M: One of whose?

W: OK, do I have your word you will not repeat any of this to anyone?

M: Yes, you have my word.

W: You promise?

M: I promise.

W: I talk with the Virgin of Guadalupe. Mother Mary. I am going through such confusing times. She told me to call you, and that we could help each other because you are one of hers. You do believe in her, right?

M: Sure, but I view her more as Mother Earth—you know, Gaia. Or Pachamama in the Incan Pantheon.

W: No, I don't! That isn't right. You're confused. But anyway, I speak with Mary all the time; she has guided me since I was young. She has helped write and promote my books, but this is a time that she alone cannot help me. I have serious health problems. I'm blocked on what I believe is going to be my most important book, and I want to do more for the world actively, but I'm unclear of my priorities, and she couldn't help me directly. She told me to call you, that you were one of hers, and that she has big plans for you, but that you are blocking yourself, and she said we could help each other.

M: Well, then, how can I help you?

W: I have an offer to do a national talk radio program to be aired at the same time as Rush Limbaugh. They think my name is big enough that I could attract all the liberals and middle-of-the-roaders that are repelled by him. But the radio show would be on daily, and my health conditions are not clear, and I need to finish this book, yet I have no energy or strength. I have to be so careful about how I eat, and I sleep much of each day.

M: Can you say no for now and do it when your health clears up and you finish the book?

W: No, it's a one-time offer: Now or not at all.

M: Can you say once or twice a week instead of daily?

W: No, five or seven days is all they will accept.

M: What if you do it with other famous liberal celebrities?

W: No, I offered. They only want me.

M: Can I help you start or fill in or write scripts or anything?

W: That's sweet, but you're not famous enough. Only me.

M: Can you prerecord each week and only do it when you are feeling strongest?

W: I did make many tapes that way. But no. They want it live.

M: Do you want to do it?

W: I thought so. But talking to you, I know I am not supposed to.

M: Are you sure? I hate Rush Limbaugh. He is one of the few people I really just can't help but hate!

W: Now I'm pretty sure. Thank you.

M: I wish you could.

W: Usually I am very strong. I have always had a will of iron and great stamina, but not with these health things.

M: What are you doing about that?

W: I see a specialist in three weeks; then I should know. I have to go. Can you make an hour to talk again if I call back?

M: Sure, any morning.

W: I'll call Wednesday.

She did call that Wednesday and three times a week for the next six weeks. Often we would talk for two or even three hours. She attempted to assist me in overcoming my blocks to becoming what she said the Virgin of Guadalupe had planned for me. She shared stories of her rise from a difficult youth to a world-renowned teacher. She gave me great advice and insights on my writing, my family, and my business. We discussed moral perspectives on abortion, political actions, Satan and the existence of true evil, world conspiracies, and her life decisions. The talks ate into my work time, but they so inspired me and were such a unique opportunity that I never minded. Then after six weeks she said, "Michael, I am going away for a very experimental operation. I am sending you a message that the Virgin Mary gave me for you to publish in *Magical Blend*. It can only be published there and only once. No one but you can ever know that I sent it to you. If I recover from this operation, I will finish my book and be more active in world politics. I'll work tirelessly to improve things. You have helped me. Remember, you are not just another human. You chose to be born on Earth in this life to assist humanity. Your soul comes from a different dimension than most human souls. You must believe in your destiny, Little Brother. Thank you for all your help. Our interactions are completed. We will return to communicating only on rare occasions. I will pray for you. Please pray for me, and believe in and pray to the Virgin of Guadalupe. She wants to help you!"

And that was it. We published the article—without her famous name attached—and I was blessed with lots of amazing advice and insights and many beliefs and pronouncements. Even today, I am unsure how I feel about it all. Clearly, she had a need to share what she knew with me. I have no doubt that she was receiving communication from an entity she believed to be the Virgin of Guadalupe, and I have no reason to doubt that it was indeed the Blessed Mother who was sending messages to me through this teacher. I can only accept these events with grace, and add this episode to my very long list called "Perks of Being the Publisher of *Magical Blend*."

Professionalism, Hard Work, and Planning

Any business, even a New Age spiritual one, must abide by the rules of professionalism and respect in order to run at its most efficient capacity. In our early years, I always believed that there would come a point when it got easier and I could coast more. I haven't found that point. We are now a large company, and our annual budgets are huge compared to what I once managed. We are sold all over the world. I have a modicum of fame and I am better able to detach and delegate. Yet I still work most days from eight in the morning to five at night at least. There always seem to be areas I care about that no one else does. Recently I haven't been as concerned about meeting payroll, but I still worry about our interpersonal dynamics and how to increase quality, effectiveness, and prosperity without being abusive to staff. I am not sure how it was in the heydays of the dot-coms, but with most small businesses, you either grow or you die. If you choose to grow, then you must be willing to adapt, evolve, and change. That requires someone holding the overview and vision and working hard to fill in the gaps and plan and prepare for the future. The good news is after 25 years I still love my work, the staff, our readers, and the information we print and share. I am a professional and a hard worker who has struggled for what I have, yet I'm always saying thanks for being blessed with such a fulfilling life.

I recently reread some of Mother Teresa's journals. I found myself relieved and empowered to discover that she had many moments when she doubted the validity of her work or the quality of her leadership. She sometimes doubted that God loved her; at other times, she even doubted God's very existence. Yet she faced down her doubts and persisted in her course, thereby setting an example that people all over the world could emulate. I am told that the biggest difference between businesses that have succeeded and those that have failed is that the successful ones persisted through the dark times of trials and setbacks. If you persist against all the challenges and disappointments, it is all but guaranteed that you will succeed. Mother Teresa is a better testimonial to that than me.

Your most important tasks in starting any new business are to take full responsibility and make time to plan. Many of us grew up in dysfunctional families. We usually bring that baggage and many bad habits to the office and our businesses. I will admit that for much of its existence, I ran *Magical Blend* from my perceived role as the head of a dysfunctional family. One of the worst aspects of that is encouraging bad employee behavior, or at least indulging it. Another is the problem of constantly fighting fires. In a dysfunctional family, someone always has a major disabling problem and everyone else either feeds into it or attempts to help. When that crisis subsides, you move on to the next one.

In a business, you can make time and set up programs to plan for a prosperous balanced future and then set up systems to head off potential problems or deal with them efficiently when they arise. If you don't do this or don't do it well, then you will be forever fighting fires and attempting to solve crises. This has been a difficult lesson for me because I so want to empower each staff member and encourage personal creativity in order to create a healthy, happy environment in which to work. However, this can easily turn into codependant support for badly performing staff. One must always be aware of the special balance, and make plans to maintain it at all times.

A successful business must get and maintain an overview. What has your business accomplished in the last five years, the last year, the last six months, and the last quarter? Did you achieve the goals that you set for the organization? Take time daily, weekly, monthly, quarterly, and annually to reexamine your company's performance and its goals, as well as your personal goals and achievements. I keep a journal and encourage everyone to do the same. Even a minimal entry looked back on a year or five years later can shed much light on what has changed and what hasn't. I personally attempt to make a prioritized "To Do" list every morning and then check over that list at the end of the day. I sit down with our financial reports each month and see how they reflect our current situation. I do an in-depth comparison to other years at the end of each quarter. And in December of every year, I reexamine the entire year, make a new plan for the upcoming one, and review and update our five-year plan. I review our business goals and objectives and my personal ones. My wife and I sit down and spend hours setting new goals for the coming year. Then we do the same thing with our children. I ask all my staff to do this as well. Then, in January, the entire staff spends a full day out of the office reviewing the year and planning the next; by the end of the day, everyone is invariably aligned with our general company-wide plans. Then I sit down and review my goals in light of all this. A business with a vision that is uppermost in employees' thoughts, and employees whose personal goals benefit from moving towards this vision is unstoppable.

Still, even with all of this hard work and planning, I have often felt more like just another worker in our organization, as opposed to the orchestra conductor I am supposed to be. I have often wondered why I didn't plan better or why I couldn't see clearly what was going on when we were in the middle of something. Yet as the years have passed, I have become easier on my self-criticism. Experience has taught me that even when things go horribly wrong, it is almost always possible to undo your mistakes and regain your perspective.

FIVE

CAN'T WE DO ANYTHING WRONG?— ISSUES 16–19 (1987)

Hello, Goodbye, and Nice to See You Again

Not surprisingly, it turned out that our little office space was too small to accommodate all the members of our growing team. We hit on a creative solution to the problem by running three work shifts during the course of the day. During that experiment, I usually got to work by 7 A.M. Jerry, Charles, and Andy arrived at 9 A.M. Jeff, Matthew, Steven Spears, and a group of volunteers came in at 5 P.M. and worked until some time late at night. Then Pat came in and did the office work from midnight until 7 or 8 A.M. We actually ran the company in this crazy way for a few months, until the system just broke down. No one could communicate with anyone else.

Fortunately for us, William and the other tech company moved out of the two-story building right around the New Year, so we began renting the entire building for not much more than we had been paying for our very cramped space. This helped out with our space limitations, but it was very much a temporary arrangement. William was planning to sell the building, and we were pretty sure that we'd be leaving as soon as he found a buyer.

From that point onward, everyone arrived between 7 A.M. and 9 A.M. and most left between 4 P.M. and 6 P.M. This proved to be much better for the organization and communication between departments. At that time, we had Charles, Jeff, and Matthew selling ads, Andy both selling ads and attempting to grow circulation, and Pat handling incoming mail, subscription fulfillment, and accounting. Pat's area was growing so fast that we bought our fourth Mac computer and hired Alice, a hard-working woman from Ireland, to help out. Then as now, I was the ringmaster, troubleshooter, planner, and vision holder. We planned to hire another advertising salesperson as soon as we found time to catch our breath.

We finally found that time after finishing issue #16 early in 1987. We hired a German gentleman, somehow appropriately named Franz, to be our new sales representative. He had sold many things and had quite a professional manner, but after his first few days on the phones, I wasn't optimistic about his chances for success. For one thing, he was the first employee we hired who didn't seem to understand *Magical Blend* enough to explain it to potential advertisers. His technique was to make tons of phone calls to big advertising firms, which in and of itself was a good thing. Upon getting someone on the phone, however, he always said, "This is Franz from the top drawer publication *Magical Blend*. We would like you to buy a large ad with us. Yes!" The implication seemed to be that if they turned him down, Franz would hunt that person down; it always sounded like he had a Luger in the top draw of his desk, ready to use at a moment's notice. It was a different approach, to say the least, but generally an unsuccessful one. We all attempted to train him in different approaches, however he would always quickly return to his two lines. He lasted a month but left us material for great jokes for years.

In the meantime, Charles's performance had badly deteriorated. It seemed that with each new staff member that we added, Charles just got worse. Although he still came through with the occasional large ad deal, his sales had become as intermittent as his attendance, neither of which was stellar. In addition, he had a weird energy that didn't really mesh with the rest of the team. Like a number of *Magical Blend* employees, both before that time and afterward, Charles didn't believe that we could stay in business without him. I have always tried to give employees a feeling of importance and a sense of ownership. I feel that everyone's opinion is worth considering and I enjoy giving credit to anyone who has an idea or takes actions that benefit the company. I also tend to be a bit indulgent of nonprofessional behavior. This style of supervising usually allows employees to excel far beyond their normal limits and achieve things they wouldn't otherwise. In some cases, however, this can create prima donnas who lose perspective of their true role. Charles thought coming in occasionally, expressing his opinion loudly, and selling a few ads made him essential. In his last meeting with Jerry and myself, the one in which we finally let him go, Charles said, "You wait and see. You will either hire me back with a big raise or you will fold. You can't do it without me." We would prove him wrong. In fact, that year of 1987 would turn out to be one of the best we had ever had.

But first, I had to deal with another readjustment and realignment in my personal life. In February my wonderful landlord, James Kong, sold the apartment house on 20th Street. It was purchased by a group of investors who took an immediate disliking to me. To get rid of me (necessary in order to push through a rent increase) they decided to move into the third floor, so Deborah and I had just two months to find a new home. A relative of Deborah's had just died and had left her a small inheritance, just right for a down payment on a house, but prices were too high then in San Francisco. After searching throughout the city and finding nothing we could afford, we discovered a lovely two bedroom house in Oakland. It was on the edge of a dangerous neighborhood but it had so much else going for it that we decided to buy it. Moving was a typical *Magical Blend* affair and it included lots of beer along with many crab and shrimp burritos. I cried when we closed the door for the last time on the third floor at 20th Street. It was tough leaving behind a place with so many great memories.

Around that time, I met John Lilly again. How he had changed since we first met during issue #3! His wife had died a couple of years before. I think that she was a great influence in keeping him healthy and on task. At that point he was around 70, yet he was dating a gorgeous 21-year-old weight lifter. I remember asking him to sum up his career. He provided a memorable answer: "Acid in the '60s, cocaine in the '70s, and ketamine in the '80s. The books tell the rest." Indeed, his books are brilliant, but also weird and somewhat difficult to follow. In his book that was out at the time, he claimed that while on ketamine he went to the realm or dimension of the silicon gods, who told him they were working to take the Earth away from humanity. Yes, John had been a pioneer and a cutting-edge thinker for decades; however, I think he might have gone a bit too far out there. He seemed to be having a difficult time translating his brilliant ideas into words that people could understand.

That spring of 1987 was an amazing time for reconnecting with famous old acquaintances. In April, I got the chance to meet Timothy Leary again. He too was a brilliant man. Just then he was working on some psychological, self-analysis computer software. This program was truly inspired; I tried it and found that it provided some fantastic insights. Yet Tim was eccentric at best. When I spoke with him, he was cynical and his thoughts were all over the place. Perhaps he was just a bit burned out. He had lots of energy and loved to achieve altered states of mind, but like Lilly, he might have been too far out to work effectively as a teacher or leader.

Bigger Offices

As the year progressed, we had 13 people working for the magazine on a regular or semi-regular basis. Therefore, it was something of a blessing in disguise when William eventually found a buyer for the office building we had been using. We had spent more than a year there at the Bryant Street office, a period in which the magazine had grown considerably. But even though the office was affordable and convenient, we needed something to push us along to the next stage of our development. So William's selling the building actually came at a perfect time as far as the magazine was concerned.

We went looking for new offices all over San Francisco. Most of the ones we liked were out of our price range or too far away from downtown. The ones that were closer and affordable were too funky or felt more like clubhouses than magazine offices. We finally found a place in the Tenderloin District, at the corner of Taylor and Market Street. This was always known as a rough neighborhood, but like everything else in San Francisco in those days, it seemed to be gentrifying rapidly. The space was on the seventh floor over the Golden Gate Theater, with the famous Fillmore West just a half block away. The San Francisco trolley turned at the corner of Market and Fifth, and the tourists waited in long lines in front of Woolworth's and Blondie's pizza, just three blocks down. All in all, the building and the neighborhood reminded me of something out of a black and white movie from the 1930s or 1940s. Humphrey Bogart would have been right at home there.

We liked the physical setup of the offices almost immediately. The doors were constructed of frosted glass with brown wood frames. There were beautiful hanging lights everywhere. The tops of the walls had intricate moldings. The view looked down on Market Street and Hyde, which was a bit seedy but always busy and exciting. Jerry liked the offices because they were nicer than most we looked at. I liked them because they had great depth and character. The lease provided for a maintenance man who emptied our trash, vacuumed, and cleaned every night of the week. There was even a doorman! This was high class for us; even better, we could almost afford it.

We signed a lease agreement with the Shorenstein Company, one of the largest property owners in San Francisco at that time. They also owned most of the city's major theaters on Geary and Market Streets. Their offices were on the third floor of our building. During our years there, we often talked to members of that ultrarich and ultrapowerful family on the elevator.

Before we left the Bryant Street building behind for good, we threw one of our by now famous potluck parties. We invited everyone we knew in the greater Bay Area to this terrific affair. The place was packed with amazing people and performances. Another great *Magical Blend* party that surely stayed in the minds of the participants for many years afterward.

After that was moving day. This was truly a team effort: Jeff, Andy, Pat, Matthew, Richard, Steven Spears, Verge Belanger, Jerry, and I all pitched in on this massive effort. We had tons of magazines, bookshelves, desks, filing cabinets, computers, chairs, and all manner of other stuff to transport. It was utter chaos.

The magazine was doing well. We were actually getting paid and paying the printers pretty much on time. We were moving into real offices. We laughed like kids as we pushed rolling chairs and dollies full of magazines out of our old place, into the U-Haul, over to our new building, up the elevator to the seventh floor, down the long hallway, around the corner, then down another long hallway to our new offices. We spread out all our stuff everywhere and anywhere. I remember that we all kept hitting our knuckles on walls and sharp edges of desks; soon there were little streaks of blood everywhere. The sun set, but I kept driving the truck back and forth from the old office to the new one, which was soon overflowing with things. I think it was about eleven at night when we unloaded the last load. Jeff, Andy, Steven, Pat, Jerry, and I were the only ones left. We sat down and shared a joint and some beer. We laughed and laughed at the day's exploits and the mess we had made of our new offices. We were worried about nothing; the future overflowed with potential and we were determined to make it ours.

We all took off the next day, which was Sunday. In fact, we took off that Monday, too. It took us about two weeks to get everything sorted out and to settle into our new digs. We were working on issue #17 at that point. It ended up coming out a few weeks off schedule, but in those days, the term "quarterly" meant that we put out an issue every three or four months. When the dust settled on our new place, Jerry, Pat, and I shared one office, Jeff, Silma Smith, and Matthew shared another, and Dylan (our new ad salesman), Richard, and Andy had the third. The fourth office served as our break/storage room, where we kept the office supplies, back issues, and the ever-important coffeemaker. Each room was connected to the one next to it and had its own door to the hallway. I had to walk by everyone to get a cup of coffee but could go down the hall the other way to the restroom with no one knowing I wasn't in the office.

Our newest addition, Dylan Van Hurst, was a Mick Jagger wannabe. He was a very good ad salesman but like so many of them, Dylan had a huge ego. He was aggressive, had some integrity issues, and very little ability for self-reflection. On top of all that, he had a cocaine habit. Dylan shared the sales office with my old friend Richard Daab, who was also selling ads at that time. His tactics were quite different from Dylan's. Richard liked to approach his leads with scenarios that were "win-win." In other words, he was looking for companies and products or services that our readers would love to buy but couldn't easily find. Richard's advertisers loved him and usually stayed on as long-term advertisers. Dylan's advertisers didn't return nearly as often. Richard was selling ads because he loved *Magical Blend* and he was teaching himself about business and sales. Richard, a health food fanatic, was always experimenting with the latest trend. One week he would be living on sauerkraut, the next poppy seeds. He spent nights meditating and was devoted to Tai Chi.

Dylan made a habit of stealing Richard's accounts whenever he thought he could get away with it. At first this caused a healthy rivalry. But as time when on, the rivalry turned into tension, then anger, then outright hostility. I often had to be the referee who had to decide who would get which accounts. I will always remember the day it reached a breaking point. We heard chairs and books smashing in the sales room. We ran back there and discovered Richard on top of Dylan. Both were draped over a tabletop and each was bleeding and punching the other hard. I yelled for them to stop but they ignored me. Then I grabbed Richard and pulled him off Dylan, while Matthew and Jeff held Dylan back. They were both screaming at each other. I told Jeff to take Dylan home and that he should take the next day off. While they were gone I calmed Richard down over lunch.

Despite all of his faults, Dylan could be rather charming. In his own way, he was also quite dedicated to the magazine. He would often come in late and work late high on coke. My sister Pat is also a night person, and despite my repeated requests, she seldom came into the office before her soap operas ended in the midafternoon. Like Dylan, however, Pat would often work late into the night. As it turned out, all that was just a setup to hide the fact that Dylan and Pat had started a secret love affair, and were sharing evenings of wild amoré in the *Magical Blend* offices. Eventually I figured it out but what was I to do? They both performed their jobs well, and I wasn't about to let either one go over a completely consensual relationship.

If We Print It, It Will Sell

Taking this office space really stretched our budget to the max. However, in those days we felt like the Microsoft of the magazine world. Circulation was growing strong and anything seemed possible. Even though we had never had such a large paid staff, we weren't in debt. We were making money, meeting famous people, throwing incredible parties, and growing by leaps and bounds. For a while there, everything we touched turned to gold. The country was hungry for New Age spiritual information and few places were providing it. From the beginning of 1985 through the summer of 1988, circulation went from 11,000 an issue (and three issues in a good year) to 75,000 an issue and seldom more than a week or two off of a quarterly schedule. If we printed it, it would sell.

Andy was as crazy as the rest of us but he had the unique ability to uncover distribution opportunities that no one could find. From these offices he convinced Waldenbooks and B. Dalton to carry us in all of their stores. At the time, they were the nation's two largest bookstore chains, with more than one thousand outlets between them. Then our growth really took off, forcing us to adjust our vision and expectation of what *Magical Blend* was and what it could be. We had only been paid to work on the magazine for three years. The hours that we worked were weird and wild. Near deadlines we would live in the office, and then after the issue got out, we'd all take off for three days or more. My sister Pat couldn't accept that I was her boss and not her little brother. She refused to come in before one in the afternoon, or else she'd miss her beloved soap operas. Then she would stay until one or two at night. Andy and Jeff preferred late mornings and late nights. I kept attempting to shepherd these renegades into normal office hours but often I would be there alone at eight or nine in the morning to unlock the doors. Sometimes I would be surprised to find someone asleep at their desk or still working straight through the night. By one in the afternoon on most days, everyone was there and we'd get some productive work done. Then someone would light a joint or buy a six-pack and the work quality would steadily deteriorate. I just hadn't yet realized that a business couldn't prosper if everyone was a multiple substance abuser.

When we ran an article by Wave Forest on the healing power of pure oxygen, I was so excited that I went out and found a place

that sold oxygen mask hook-ups and then went to a welding supply company and purchased a large tank of oxygen for the office.
It was not only supposed to be great for health, but it promised to
increase energy and alertness and help people recover from hang-
overs. For that last reason, mainly, oxygen got a workout by our
staff. Eventually our bodies developed a high level of oxidation
and the effects became all but unnoticeable. Of course, by then
the novelty factor had worn off, so I attempted to return the items
for refunds. Unsuccessfully, I might add.

That was life at *Magical Blend* in those days—lots of experimentation with all sorts of substances and behaviors. Personally, I
have come to the realization that marijuana (our drug of choice
back then) makes me too paranoid. It makes me talk about what
I am going to do, but I seldom do as much as I talk about and it
does not help me realize my ambitions. I eventually gave it up and
am glad to say I now drink much less alcohol as well. I seldom do
any substances except for coffee and the occasional beer or two
and ritual substances in Peru and the like. I figure that the best
gift I can give myself, the business, my children, and the staff is to
model good, professional behaviors. Not that many of them notice
much, but I still make every attempt to lead through example and
these days no one drinks or does drugs during work hours.

Magical Blend has allowed me to explore many spiritual practices, including meditation, ritual, self-hypnosis, chanting, light
and sound machines, fasting, intense prayer, and many extreme
religious and spiritual practices, as well as the wisdom of indige-
nous peoples and a powerful array of shamanic practices. Thus, it
has become relatively easy for me to enter altered states of mind,
body, or spirit at will. It is wonderful when a spiritual pilgrim or
searcher reaches the conclusion that all magical tools and gizmos,
including substances, are fine when used wisely. However, practice, research, persistence, and focused intent are really the only
requirements needed to achieve any goal. That includes a state of
bliss, becoming one with God, accessing lost wisdom, astral travel-

ing, and even parlor tricks such as reading minds or sending someone a clear telepathic message.

Drugs, substance use, and substance abuse were an important part of the 1960s, 1970s, and 1980s. They represented a common ground where otherwise unconnected staff members could meet during *Magical Blend*'s early years. Yet we must always hope that the pain and failures that aging and experience give us lead to a higher wisdom and a putting aside of our childish props.

An exciting event occurred that spring. Joseph Campbell, who wrote the definitive books about the impact that myths and archetypes have on all our lives, planned to give a talk at the Palace of Honor about the Grateful Dead and their place in myth. Andy in particular was really looking forward to that one, so we got some press passes and went. It was an exquisite talk from a brilliant man. Afterward, we went up to the podium and told Joseph that we had recorded his address. We asked if we could turn it into an article. He was very warm and agreeable. We hung out with him and a group of folks and asked questions for an hour until he graciously bade us all a good night. I'm proud to say that we featured Joseph Campbell in *Magical Blend* two years before Bill Moyers made him world famous.

Not long after the Campbell talk, Van Ault and I met with Jack Pursel, whom I hadn't seen in quite a few years. It is always interesting to revisit people from your past and see how they have changed. When we first encountered Jack, back during the days of issue #4, he was a humble businessman who channeled the entity named Lazaris on the side. By this time, Lazaris was a big star and Jack had retreated almost into the background. But not quite. Lazaris had a huge following and Jack was something of a despot. It always seemed to me that most channels and psychics, like Ramtha or Mafu, usually provided simple platitudes and basic commonsense advice. The perspectives and agendas all seemed very affected by the person doing the channeling. Yet that being said I will always treasure one thing Ramtha once said. He said, "I have looked everywhere for the devil or Satan or Lucifer. I have searched in the center of the earth and the sun and other dimensions and the far corners of the universe. I have only found him in the hearts and minds of those poor people who believe in him. I can firmly state he exists nowhere else in all of creation!" Unfortunately, precious little of what I heard from Lazaris compared with this kind of wisdom. Still, it was good to see Jack again.

That summer, I had the chance to speak with Douglas Adams and Saul Bellow. Wow, what creative guys! They had both made it so big that most people appeared as fawning fans to them. In cases such as this, I always attempt to be nonfawning and to treat them as an equal would. They both responded well to that approach. However, you can tell when someone is almost too famous to be real. They were guarded in what they said and somewhat aloof. Well, perhaps I will have their challenges some day.

I got to meet Jean Houston for the first time that October. Her book *The Search for the Beloved* was absolutely wonderful. Jean was equally wonderful. I found her to be brilliant, yet warm and unimposing. She operated a mystery school with her husband and fellow author, Robert Masters. In *The Search for the Beloved,* she wrote, "The best gift our parents give us is their mistakes and weakness and the times they disappoint us. When we heal from these disappointments, these secret wounds, we are from then forth able to heal from whatever the world can do to us." I felt as though Jean was a good new friend who would be there when we needed her. She was also on a mission to help build a better tomorrow, and in that task we were and are still allies.

Different Magic

Ever since we had started working full time on *Magical Blend,* Jerry and I would begin our workday with a morning affirmation and visualization ritual. We would sit on the floor, close our eyes, and do the ritual each morning. It was generally quite brief, but over time, as we hired staff and we made attendance mandatory, some were uncomfortable with this ritual. So we made it optional. Those who chose not to participate were free to do their work instead. Yet even that felt like pressure and an imposition to our open-minded, free-spirited staff. Jerry and I took to running our little ritual early on Mondays and after work hours on Wednesdays and Fridays. Still the staff felt weirded out by it and feared that I planned to turn *Magical Blend* into a church or a cult. So the affirmations and visualizations and rituals have become a personal and private activity, which I share only on special occasions. I regret this for I strongly believe that all those prayers and ceremonies, done in earnestness and with full hearts, were a big reason for our amazing success.

The changing nature of our ritual reflected other things that were going on with the magazine. Business-wise, this was the point in our history when *Magical Blend* was one of the very few New Age magazines in the marketplace. There were even fewer resources for cutting-edge, California style spiritual insights and information. It was a heady time, and our successes throughout 1987 finally confirmed my long-standing belief that we were a real business that could make it in the big, tough world of magazine publishing. We all assumed that we were just blessed and that our success was meant to be. I did my best to steer the ship; however, more than half of the staff had been volunteers and the other half were mostly poets, artists, musicians, and writers—not the most disciplined office employees, to say the least. In those days, as I have stated, we tolerated people using (and abusing) their substance of choice, even during working hours. So people smoked marijuana, drank alcohol, snorted cocaine, did speed or heroin, you name it. It was a strange office for damn sure. If I had only known then that businesses almost all have cycles of growth and contraction and that every successful endeavor eventually gets imitated, I might have run things differently. However, I had never operated a business before, so we just spent what we made as we went. We gave people healthy raises and purchased large meals for the staff on a regular basis. I had to learn the hard way that although businesses can be run like a family or a group of friends, if no one is responsible then no one is responsible.

There was a different kind of magic at work at *Magical Blend* at that time. Over our first few years, we were focused on survival. We put issues out whenever we could and however we could. The most important thing was that we continued to get this important material and empowering information out to the world at large. Slowly, as we figured out what we were doing and started to turn *Magical Blend* into a business, the priorities began to change in a subtle way. Our message and our mission stayed the same, but the way in which we accomplished things had to undergo an adjustment. I had to adapt first, by taking on the mantle of responsibility and organization, both of which I resisted greatly. By 1987, we had steady and expanding revenue streams, but those were matched and even exceeded by increased expenditures in rent, payroll, printer bills, phone charges, postage, food, parties, and lots else. Although many members of the staff were still somewhat cavalier about schedules and professionalism, they were still much better than the volunteers from the wild days of the early 1980s.

As the year came to an end, I remember thinking that we were right on the cusp of truly great things. I had always been proud of the magazine and the people who worked on it, but now we were entering a stage where wealth, fame, and influence seemed to be ours for the taking. I was in my mid-thirties, healthy, focused, and intense. All of my dreams were coming true. Looking back on it now, maybe I was filled with hubris. Maybe our reach exceeded our grasp, if only by a little. Maybe we moved too aggressively in taking advantage of the opportunities that presented themselves to us.

For the moment, however, 1987 was certainly among the best of times, for *Magical Blend* and for myself. The year 1988 would prove to be something different altogether.

SIX

CAN'T WE DO ANYTHING RIGHT?—
ISSUES 20–23 (1988)

International Distribution

I should have known right from the beginning that 1988 was going to be a struggle. Shortly after we returned from our New Year holiday, Andy quit. He felt overworked and was very resentful toward me and the rest of the staff. I would work with Andy very differently today than I did then. I would help him set limits and keep things in perspective. However, at the time, I was so focused on the important work that he was doing in growing our circulation that I encouraged him to keep at it. Finally he could take no more. He was a complicated guy, but Andy had skills that we really ended up missing.

I took over distribution in Andy's place and hired a former employee from Fred Finch, Brad Pethoud, to help with all the duties associated with that department—record keeping, billing and collecting, data entry, etc. Brad had been a Russian Orthodox monk and was a numerologist. He was great with details. Almost immediately after hiring Brad, I signed an agreement with our first truly national distributor, who talked about taking huge numbers of copies and placing them in stores across the nation. With that as a feather in our cap, I opened negotiations with various distributors in Australia, Canada, Europe, Japan, South America, and Hong Kong. It was a matter of striking while the iron was hot. Andy had started some of this stuff, but once I got going, I decided to expand his work and take it up to the sky!

It didn't take long before we had signed agreements in place to distribute *Magical Blend* all over the world. What a dream come true! Our distribution went through the roof, and everyone in the office was infused with a very real sense that *this was it!* It seemed as though we would all be rich and famous by the end of the year. I was confident that once readers saw *Magical Blend,* they would respond by buying it right away, regardless of the language they spoke or the information that they were seeking.

Meanwhile, we continued to add quality people to our staff. Yuka Hirota started as one of four paid interns from the San Francisco Academy of Art. We placed Matthew Courtway in charge of supervising these interns, who truly came from all four corners of the globe. One was from Ethiopia, one was from Arkansas, one was from New Orleans, and Yuka came to us from Japan. The first three had the work habits of typical art school students—lack of focus, bad punctuality and attendance, and the general sense that they really didn't want to work. Well, interns are sometimes a hit or miss proposition. With Yuka, we hit a home run. She stood out right away as being quiet but very self-disciplined. She loved *Magical Blend,* fully supported our mission, and was willing to take on any responsibility we assigned to her. Our internships started in January. By May the other three interns were long gone, but we hired Yuka on a full-time basis for the summer. In just a few brief months with us, she had already systematized our subscription renewal mailings, organized the sending of sample copies to readers, and assisted in the overall design of the magazine. She had her capable fingers into many aspects of what we were doing and improved whatever she touched. As summer progressed, she and Matthew began dating and by fall they were living together.

Around this time my sister Nancy and her husband had agreed to divorce. They had for years headed up a very cutting-edge organic farm for a spiritual community in Colorado. However, she decided to start anew and moved to San Francisco. Jerry let me hire her and she was a joy to have in the office. She helped out greatly during that chapter of transition. She has always been a very important character in my life. She had even contributed an article to our first issue. I enjoyed the unique perspective she brought to *Magical Blend* for that short time.

At the end of a particularly prosperous week, we would have a little Friday afternoon tradition. I would drive down to the Mission District and pick up crab burritos for the whole staff at a small Mexican restaurant (long since closed) called La Fiesta. Then I would buy four six-packs of good beer. We would stop work at 2 P.M. and all sit together in Jerry's and my part of the office and eat and drink and laugh and then call it a week. One such afternoon a reporter for the *L.A. Times* called. He was doing research for an article on why whales and dolphins were held in such high regard by the New Age community. I had had a couple of beers and felt playful so I stated that cetaceans were seen as more intelligent and spiritual than humans and were replacing priests, rabbis, and ministers. I never suspected that they would quote me in the *L.A. Times* or that the article would be reprinted in every small town newspaper from Anchorage to Cape Cod. This recognition, as bizarre as it was, brought about a nice surge in subscription orders. Life seemed weird, blessed, and simple in those days.

Many Unhappy Returns

Unfortunately, the wild circulation growth of that year didn't turn out as we had hoped. By the middle of that summer, my garage in Oakland was filled with thousands of extra copies of issues #20 and #21, which we had overprinted in hopes of massive newsstand reorders. However, it became painfully clear that the term "reorder" was not in the vocabulary of our new national and international distributors. To make matters worse, the additional newsstand sales that we did manage to generate did not translate into large numbers of new subscribers. Our new major domestic distributor placed our magazine in Piggly Wiggly groceries as well as Winn Dixie stores throughout the Bible Belt. As a result, we received a great deal of fundamentalist Christian hate mail, plus a ton of returned copies that just didn't sell in those stores.

By the end of August, the proverbial shit hit the fan. After sending our national distributor almost one hundred thousand copies, he sent us a check for $500. Then we got a notice stating that the distributor was declaring bankruptcy. Following that, the company's owner dropped off the face of the earth. I put a collection agency on him but it was useless. On top of that, the Australian distributor cut their order from over 10,000 copies to just 400; they claimed to have a 98 percent return rate on the initial copies that we sent them. It was the same story in Europe, as our print order there fell from 20,000 to 600. The Canadian order dropped from 10,000 to 1,000. We collected very tiny amounts of money from all of these foreign distributors. The orders in Japan, Hong Kong, and Mexico were small, so we weren't planning on getting very much money from them anyway. But I had been holding the printer and all our other creditors at bay waiting for payment from these distributors. Now there was no money coming and the bills were piling up. I started to lose sleep at night, trying to figure out how to keep the business afloat. Only one option presented itself, and it was one that I didn't even want to contemplate: laying off the staff. As time went by, however, that seemed to be our only chance for survival.

It was a Monday afternoon early in September when Jerry and I called a staff meeting. Without any fanfare or excess drama, we simply gave everyone the news that *Magical Blend* was in serious financial trouble, and that in order to keep it alive, only Matthew, Yuka, Pat, Jerry, and I would be staying on at minimum wage. Try as I might, I couldn't keep myself from crying as I laid off my sister Nancy, Jeff, Dylan, Richard, Brad, and the other five staff members. At the end of this somber day, Jeff announced that he was going to have a layoff party at his home that Friday. That proved that this crew would party for any reason. I dreaded going but decided that it was only right to attend.

The party was bittersweet. It was sad knowing that an era had ended. Everyone was understanding and forgiving except Dylan, who got terribly drunk during the course of the evening. He blamed me for mismanagement and bad judgment and in front of everyone yelled, "Michael, you are a terrible businessman! You misled us and now you've ruined our lives." I was shocked, saddened, and angry at his hurtful words. I replied angrily, "Shut up, Dylan! You are a selfish, incompetent, mean asshole!" Then, with tears in my eyes, I walked to a different part of Jeff's house. Deborah and I left soon after, but the pain of the layoffs and that party haunted me for months.

At the time, I felt like a terrible failure. But after dealing with those feelings, I realized that with wise work and some massive penny-pinching, we might still save the business. I knew that Dylan was wrong and that I had done the best that I could. Now the five of us had agreed to stay at less than minimum wage. We felt it was our chance to keep the dream alive. We dug in and worked as hard, smart, and efficiently as we could. We all agreed to do whatever needed to be done. I started to make advertising sales calls again. However, as the publisher, everyone wanted me to do them a favor: print their story, or their mother's painting, or their nephew's poetry. Most wanted their business to be spotlighted in an interview or article about them. When I attempted to tell them we didn't do that sort of editorial they said, "Well, can't you change your policy? You're the publisher, aren't you?"

After two weeks of this I had sold some ads but made more people angry. On Friday, I left the office discouraged. That weekend while watching *Star Trek* reruns at home in Oakland it hit me. James Tiberius Kirk was really William Shatner. Of course! I would become a character. I would be Neal Tiberius Powers: Neal T. Powers, ad salesman extraordinaire! Neal, I decided, had grown up in New York. He was aggressive and could be a bit abrasive when necessary. He was a childhood friend of Michael's. Neal was a great salesman, but unfortunately for his advertising clients, the publisher and editor would not allow him any influence over editorial.

That Monday, I had business cards printed and redid all my sales promotion letters. Neal was born. He had none of the problems Michael did and was a much better salesperson. But the "T" made the stage name too obvious. People kidded Neal, saying, "Kneel to what powers?" I quickly dropped the T and became an ad sales machine. I would get to the office at 4:30 A.M., would make ad calls until the midafternoon, and then turn back into Michael the publisher from then until late into the evenings. I would often sleep in the office or drive home, crawl into bed in Oakland beside a sleeping Deborah, catch four hours or so of shut-eye, get up, shower, and drive back. It took me a couple weeks longer than it usually took Dylan and Richard, but I filled issue #22 with ad commitments and waited joyously for them to arrive. But I had never done this before and I didn't get signed contracts, credit cards, or even a promised arrival date for the materials. Only one-third of the committed ads arrived; I called all the others and most said that they had changed their minds. We had to hold the issue while I resold two-thirds of the ads. I began working Saturdays and Sundays, but I refilled the issue with paying advertisers, and we eventually sent it off to the printer.

Although Neal was a great boon to *Magical Blend*, Deborah hated him. She said he was actually was a more aggressive, darker, possessed, driven side of me. She forbade him to come into our home! "If you can't learn to turn Neal off and bring Michael's personality to the top, then don't bother coming home," she would say to me. We took to fighting on the rare occasions when we were awake and alone together. I was exhausted and focused on keeping *Magical Blend* alive. She missed me and would have preferred to see the magazine pass away and me get a dependable job as a high school teacher or in someone else's company. I resented her for that. Things got worse between us. We were both unrealistically paranoid that the other was having an affair. One day, after I closed two great ad deals, I went out for a walk in the Tenderloin District around our office. There was an apartment for rent sign on this nearby, high-rise apartment complex. I went in and checked it out. Because the neighborhood was kind of rough, the rent was cheap. I didn't deliberate for long. Right then and there, I signed a lease and got a key to a 14th-floor apartment with a great view of the city. The next day, I drove to Oakland while Deborah was at work and loaded all of my books, journals, and keepsakes into my van. I left her a note saying that I was sorry but that I just couldn't stand the fighting any more. I got a mattress off the street and bought a used coffee maker, a pot, a frying pan, a few utensils, and some lamps. I now could sleep two extra hours a night without any fighting. Neal had taken over. He had won, leaving Michael's life in splinters. Deborah called, but I asked her not to do so anymore. I was done with our relationship. For the next several months, I had no social life—just the magazine and sleep.

What was a day like when I first became Neal? I would stop at one or another all-night restaurant for a quick breakfast of eggs, home fries, and toast. I would arrive at the office by 4:30 A.M. so I could get everything ready to call the East Coast businesses beginning at 5 A.M. my time, which of course was 8 A.M. for them. Then I would attempt to call as many businesses as I could, sometimes 75 in an hour. I was always looking for businesses that had products or services that our readers would benefit from and probably couldn't find anywhere else. It usually took me 150 calls to get an ad commitment, and then another six or seven calls to work out all of the details. I also had to track my calls and send out my media kits. Then I would have to make sure the ad copy arrived, along with payments. I know it sounds archaic now, but our computers were just used for word processing, database management, and layouts. We didn't own a fax machine; few companies at the time did. Of course, e-mail was still only for the military. I had to ensure that the advertisers gave the OK to any ad that Matthew or Yuka designed. Then I had to instruct Matthew and Yuka where to place the ads in the magazine.

Jerry handled all of the editorial other than my "Potentials" column and a few other interviews or articles that I did. The year that I was Neal, Neal was the entire advertising department, so it was understandable that I did less writing that year than any other. In the early years of *Magical Blend*, I would agonize over my "Potentials" column for a week or two. Well, I no longer had that luxury. I would sit in my apartment over the course of one morning, and give myself a three-hour deadline to write the best 1,000 words I could muster. I then passed the column along to Jerry and had him edit it to the best of his ability.

Pat maintained the subscriber base, covered the distribution, and handled our income. Yuka did all the resubscription notices on her own in-house. Jerry wrote and edited most of the magazine, and Matthew and Yuka put it all together beautifully. Matthew and Yuka were for the first time able to redefine the unique layout and graphic approach which set *Magical Blend* magazine in a class all its own for most of the next decade. In countless ways, if it weren't for these four individuals and their extraordinary dedication and determined, high-quality, ceaseless work, *Magical Blend* would have ceased to exist that year. Without each of them and all they were willing to do, it would not have mattered the slightest bit what I had done.

I never stopped for lunch anymore and only left the office when absolutely necessary. With just five dedicated staff members, supervision and payroll became quite simple. I interfaced with the printer and the largest distributors. These were the wholesalers who place our magazine in chains and independent bookstores. We also always kept a service to any bookstore who preferred to deal with us directly. We probably serviced somewhere between 500 and 1,000 bookstores in this way. In the evenings after 5 P.M., I called Hawaii for possible sales, made my media kits, prepared for the next workday, and looked over the work that Pat, Jerry, Matthew, and Yuka had done during the day. I always kept an eye on expenses and income, and searched to make sure that we were getting the best prices on paper, office supplies, printing, and whatever else we needed to purchase. Before I left the office most nights I would attempt to pray and visualize growing sales, increased prosperity, and a joyous work place. Usually I would leave the office between midnight and 1 A.M., sleep for a few hours, and then do it all again the next day. After a few months, I did once again try to take Sundays off.

Who Has AIDS?

At the end of 1988, Jerry's partner Bill was diagnosed with HIV. Bill had been fearful of this dreaded disease for years, almost to the point of obsession. Now he had it, back in the days when such a diagnosis was generally a death sentence. Jerry and Bill planned a trip to England for a month to celebrate life. The day before they were to leave, Jerry, too, was diagnosed with HIV. Almost as soon as they returned from England, Bill became seriously ill, and Jerry became his full-time, exclusive nurse. For the next year and a half, as Bill's condition worsened, Jerry spent much of his energy taking care of his lover. He continued to handle his responsibilities at *Magical Blend* in a most professional manner, but his heart and soul were understandably dedicated to the care of Bill.

After the layoffs, Richard Daab had stayed as an unpaid roving reporter. Richard knew that I was in shock that Jerry had HIV. I was devastated—the thought of losing one of my best friends and business partner was unthinkable. To try to cheer me up, Richard got passes to the Cirque du Soleil, the Quebec nonanimal circus. We were trying to figure out an angle to write an article about them. Sitting in the front row and having press passes unwittingly made us part of the show. They threw water on us and made us run around. It was hilarious. After the show we got to go back to the performer's tent and talk with them. They were sweet and funny, warm and caring. We shared a drink of wine as they told us the history and evolution of their unique circus. Afterward, as we drove away, I was thankful for Richard's friendship and that there was so much laughter in the world. Then I thought of the terrible illness that Bill and Jerry shared and I cried and prayed for their lives. Jerry was one of the closest, dearest friends I had ever had. He had been a fantastic business partner and I just loved the man as I do my family. I prayed to whatever powers would listen, offering to take years off of my own life, if necessary, if only Jerry could enjoy many more good, healthy years.

After the layoffs, we were a small, dedicated, and focused team. We banned all drugs and alcohol from the office, got rid of the oxygen tank and every other superficial expense, and generally ran a lean and mean operation. Matthew, Pat, Yuka, Jerry, and I were all putting in 10- and 12-hour days. Everyone was getting paid $200 a week without exception. We were working hard but keeping everything together. Then our tightly wound little ball of twine began to fray. Bill's AIDS worsened, and he was hospitalized. His doctors gave him just a limited time to live, and Jerry seemed to lose hope. He cut back on his time in the office, but he held to his commitments and even did lots of extra work at home. However, Bill's condition continued to worsen and Jerry was feeling sick a lot, as well. This meant that the remaining four of us had to step up and do even more.

We did our best. Every one of us took on portions of the work that Jerry had been doing, but since we were already stretched thin, it was difficult. Pat became moody; she was tired of being overworked and underpaid. We argued increasingly in the office. Like Deborah, Pat didn't like Neal. Just when I thought I would go crazy with her insults and demands, she became sick with a uterine infection that caused her excruciating pain. Fortunately, we had kept up our health coverage, because Pat needed to be admitted to the hospital for two weeks of observation. The doctors eventually had to operate and remove her uterus. Matthew, Yuka, Jerry, and I all visited her in the hospital a few days after the surgery. She looked at us all and laughed. She said, "I love all of you and the magazine, but I can't do it any more. I am resigning. I will go on worker's comp, and you should hire two people to take my place." We tried to talk her out of it but not too convincingly. Pat's career with *Magical Blend* was over.

Does the Magic Still Work?

Although our budget was tight, we knew that replacing Pat was a must. We had heard of a military program called Swords to Plowshares, which allowed you to interview ex-GIs for jobs in your company. The military would pay the candidate you chose for the first six months of their tenure, as long as you agreed to pay them for six months afterward. That's how Bingo started working for our company. He had just finished a four-year hitch with the Navy in which he toured the world. Bingo grew up in Detroit but fell in love with San Francisco and wanted to settle down there. He was a Baptist and went to church every Sunday, but he also drank and smoked dope whenever he wasn't working. Bingo was charming, brilliant, efficient, hard-working, fast-learning, and, most of all, thrilled to get the job. He wasn't Pat but he was the best person we could have ever imagined to do a similar job. When Pat resigned, I was depressed and fearful of failure. When we hired Bingo, I was joyous. It felt like a new chapter was beginning.

One morning toward that winter, I went to get my old beat up Chevy van, which I had taken to parking on the streets of the Tenderloin, and found that it had been torched. In fact, it was burned to a black husk! Now I couldn't leave San Francisco, even if I had the time or desire. Which I certainly did not.

A couple of weeks later, I was having lunch with Pat, who had pretty much recovered from her illness and surgery. Pat told me that she had gone to Oakland recently, where she and Deborah had shared dinner. It seemed that Deborah really missed me and was taking courses at the world-renowned Berkeley Psychic Institute to better understand me, my interests, and what had gone wrong in our relationship. She had never been seeing anyone else and wished I would call her. She had a better perspective on my business problems now.

About then, a woman by the name of Daisy dropped by the office looking for a day job. She loved *Magical Blend* and had been reading it for years. Daisy was a practicing witch who belonged to a San Francisco coven. She had a lot of desire to work with us, but I informed her that all I could offer was a commission-only job selling ads. She accepted.

It turned out that Daisy had a boyfriend, and they lived in North Beach. He had his own demanding job and was obviously very open-minded, because most nights she danced in a strip joint and turned tricks on the side. I guess you could say we had a high-class hooker as Neal Powers' first advertising sales trainee. She was seductive on the phones, which wasn't a surprise. What was surprising was that within weeks, she was selling half the ads in the magazine. I could breathe, think, and be Michael again, at least more of the time.

We also hired a new assistant for Jerry. Her name was Julie Marchasin and she was talented, enthusiastic, a hard worker, and a breath of fresh air. Julie added so much to *Magical Blend* and our new chapter which was then unfolding. However, for me one of the most wonderful things she did started one morning when she came to the office early—not just early for her, but early for everyone! She was there at 7:30 A.M., all excited about a series of tapes that she had been listening to. Julie was inspired by and in awe of the women who made them. She believed that this woman, who was the director of the C. G. Jung Center for Education and Research, had an important message and we needed to help her get it out. The woman was Dr. Clarissa Pinkola Estes, one of the best storytellers and most insightful geniuses that I have ever been exposed to. I had to give Julie my OK to contact Dr. Estes and turn her tape of the *Stone Child* into an article. We had to do this at once because Julie was sure that Dr. Estes would soon be too famous to talk to us. Well, that project took more time than most of our articles, because Julie felt strongly about what it needed to say and Dr. Estes felt equally strong about what the message should be. That month we had quite a telephone bill to Colorado, where Dr. Estes was based. However, when Julie finished it was a great piece and Dr. Estes had become *Magical Blend*'s and my friend. The next year, her world-changing best-seller *Women Who Run with the Wolves* came out and, as Julie predicted, Dr. Estes became famous and in demand everywhere. The book set records on the best-seller lists and changed many people's lives. Yet, Clarissa has remained an important friend. She has contributed to *Magical Blend* a lot over the years and we have enjoyed many long conversations. She has given me some of the best inspiration and advice I have ever received. I was extremely lonely at the time, and I caught myself developing a crush on both Julie and Clarissa. But I had sworn after the wild volunteer years not to have relationships with people involved with *Magical Blend*, so I nipped those interests in the bud and retained them as friends and confidantes.

Life was improving; I even took a weekend off to catch up on my sleep. When I woke up, I realized how lonely and empty my life was without Deborah. I gave her a call and asked her out for dinner. Of course, since my van was no longer operational, she had to make the trip over to San Francisco. We shared a lovely Vietnamese dinner where she told me all about the Berkeley Psychic Institute. Then she came back to my apartment. By the next morning, we were dating again. After three weeks of seeing each other most nights and spending much of the weekends together, I decided to buy Yuka's Toyota Corolla. She let me have it for a good price. She had to sell it because the city was about to seize it for overdue traffic and parking tickets. It was a great little car that served me for years. Thus I regained my mobility and ended the year spending most of my time with Deborah back at our old place in Oakland.

Businesses Have Cycles

Spiritually and business-wise, the year 1988 represented *Magical Blend*'s first dose of reality. All living things go through periods of expansion and periods of contraction. It's no different for businesses. We basically expanded from 1980 until 1988, and then we contracted in a big way. After our national and international distributors' debacle, we found ourselves with a debt that was, to our little business, staggering. We responded by laying off most of the staff, reducing everyone else's wages, cutting all expenditures to the bone, and focusing on stabilization and healing.

We had five dedicated, hardworking, and efficient people working as a unified team; when one fell out we were blessed to find a qualified replacement. We all expanded our responsibilities and kept our focus on the goal. By the spring of 1989, we felt safe enough to begin hiring other new staff assistants, ad salespeople, office help, and editorial assistants. We did this slowly and wisely. We ended the year 1989 with money in the bank and all debts paid off. Then we continued to expand slowly until 1991, when we went through new changes.

Many businesses fail when they experience an unforeseen contraction after years of growth. Many times, such swings between good times and bad are inevitable. Yet ultimate success is still possible if an organization remembers the importance of adaptability, a willingness to sacrifice, and a belief in the vision and the future. In business, as in life, experiencing a setback or an outright failure is the worst time to give up. Actually, failure is a great opportunity to learn about who you are, what your business is made of, what you did wrong, and how you can learn from your mistakes so that you don't make the same errors again.

Immediately after the great San Francisco earthquake of 1906, when most businesses were in total disarray and people everywhere were traumatized, the founders of the Bank of America dug out the safes that were buried in their crumbled building and dragged them down to the wharfs. There they placed signs that read, "Let's rebuild San Francisco! Cash loans available here." Every disaster offers opportunities for growth and great wealth; it is up to each of us to decide how much we want it.

Magical Blend has always been about how our mundane world overflows with magic and mystery, if we only allow ourselves to become aware of it. Our thoughts, words, and deeds are the most powerful tools for manifestation imaginable, yet we generally under use them. I don't want to mislead anyone with the impression that it is powerful to just think nice thoughts or that if you daydream and wish for things they will simply manifest. I have met people who claim to lead magical lives in which they never have to do anything they don't want to. However, my personal experience has been that it takes a concerted effort to manifest anything worthwhile. If nothing else, I have discovered that the gods and goddesses have a sense of humor. If I set my goals on something, I must work to marshal my thoughts, intentions, and words before I begin to take the appropriate actions. At that point the universe tends to throw me a curve. Some other opportunity comes up, or the reason why I wanted to achieve the goal shifts.

Manifestation is also about passion and a willingness to adapt. If you passionately want to accomplish or manifest something and you are willing to do whatever it takes to achieve that end, then you will reach your objective. A problem that most people have is that they are afraid and unsure. If you let those things stop you, then you will never manifest anything. We are all afraid and we are all unsure. It's not about being those things; it's about what you do with those feelings. The best thing to do is to acknowledge them and then to take the risks involved to go for the next step. If you are knocked down or trip, don't give up and don't feel like a failure, just know that it is all part of the mystery and magic required for the manifestation. Setbacks, rejection, pain, and disappointment don't mean that you are a failure or that you will never manifest what you want. It's all part of the process. You must pick yourself out of the mud, brush yourself off, and adapt and persist until you manifest what you want. We all must remember that we are miraculous, magical beings. The majority of our makeup is a mystery; we don't know why we have so much seemingly unutilized DNA material or why we only appear to use a small percentage of our brains. What we do know is that throughout history, determined people have accomplished awe-inspiring things. We have to believe that each of us is capable of that as well.

Taking full responsibility for creating our lives is a difficult thing for most of us. Heck, taking responsibility for *anything* is difficult for most people. It is so much easier to blame others than to assume our own power and admit we have not been attentive to what we have manifested in our lives. This could be where the magic and the mystery come in. If magic is real, then why doesn't our world look more like Middle Earth and why do we rely on pollution-producing transportation and science to get things done?

Well, magic is real, and its essence is mystery. At its root is manifestation. For what good is magic if it is just meaningless ritual or ceremony? To achieve change, we need to think, talk, and act. Seldom do we align these three aspects of our being and seldom do we focus them clearly with intent on what we want to magically manifest in our lives. As you think, as you speak your desires, and as you act upon them, you will be able to manifest positive results in your life. Most of us spend our time worrying about what we don't want to happen; in actuality, many times doing this actually draws those things into our lives. We don't have to stop all worrying nor do we have to be vigilant of our thoughts every second. What we do have to do is begin considering that our goals and expectations can be aligned and thus will be more likely to manifest what we are working toward.

To me, this screams of far-flung magic and exquisite mysteries, and whispers of what manifestation is in our reality. No, Dorothy, you don't have to go to Oz to find witches or wizards—you just have to look into your own dusty Kansas mirror, for you and every one of us in truth is able to manifest magic. Anyone, and I do mean anyone, can manifest a life overflowing with magic, joy, and ecstatic living. I thoroughly believe that if we want to minimize negative events, then we just have to manifest a better reality for ourselves. Now wouldn't that be a mysterious and magical mega-manifestation! *Magical Blend*'s continued success proves that, together, we can change the course of history. Together, I believe, we will cocreate a wonderful Ecotopian society on Earth in the next 50 years. All we need to do is begin.

SEVEN

THE BIGGEST CHANGES—ISSUES 24–42 (1989–1993)

Joy and Tears

As 1989 opened, we began to emerge from the wreckage of our overblown dreams. We did this by publishing trimmed-down issues of *Magical Blend* and slashing expenses wherever and whenever possible. All of our penny-saving sacrifices bore fruit by the end of the winter. We had eaten down much of our debt, and circulation and ad sales were starting to rebound. We were getting paid by the distributors for two-thirds of the copies that we sent them. That was much better than before. We hired a woman named Amy, a pre-law student, to help in the office. She and Richard Daab quickly embarked on a passionate relationship.

By then I had given up my small San Francisco apartment and had moved back to Oakland. A month later I asked Deborah to marry me. She accepted, with one stipulation—that we have chil-

128

dren. Wow, that took me aback. A family—us? And me, a father? It had finally become clear to me that I wanted to spend the rest of my life with Deborah, but at that time I wasn't sure about bringing more children into the world, or the responsibilities that came with raising them, either. So I went off on a vision quest for a week in Death Valley and fasted and meditated on the question. When I returned, I consented to making a family with Deborah, so long as we adopted the children. Deborah agreed, and we set the wedding date for June 13. Deborah also agreed to let me work 12-hour days at *Magical Blend*, providing that I held it to 12 hours and took off on Sundays to share my time with her.

From that point forward, Neal and the other ad sales people sold like fiends, generating solid advertising revenues and keeping the business moving forward. We were steadily working away at our debt. (In fact, in the spring of 1989, we each took a small raise.)

The wedding was fabulous. I was blessed to have two wonderful best men: Jerry and my old Boy Scout buddy from Massachusetts, David Himmer, whom I had known since we were 11. Many other friends and family members came out from the East Coast to attend. Lots of people Deborah and I knew or had worked with came and most of the *Magical Blend* staffs from our first decade were there in one way or another. Jeff Fletcher, Matthew Courtway and Yuka Hirota's music group, Cardinal Sin, performed as our wedding band. Steven Spears volunteered to be our cameraman. Looking back at that wedding reception now, from a distance of 15 years, I realize that it was the last *Magical Blend* party of the early days. In many ways, it marked the end of our wild, crazy, and formative first decade and the beginning of our next chapter, one that was more grounded and mature, yet still unorthodox and nonconformist. Those early years were in some way our most picturesque. We were young people, living and working in the big city. We had a dream, lots of creativity, boundless enthusiasm, little money, and big plans. The adventures shared by me and the *Magical Blend* staffs prior to 1989 were wonderful and amazing. But by the time of my wedding, things had changed, and those changes were about to accelerate. Living with *Magical Blend* was not just about fun and games and drugs and parties anymore.

At that point, I felt great about almost everything in my life and my business. I felt so great, in fact, that Deborah and I took a three week honeymoon in Mexico, exploring the Yucatan and many Mayan ruins. While there, I managed to open some bookstores in Cancun and Mexico City and write my column. Even on my honeymoon, thoughts of the magazine were never far away.

When I returned, Amy and Daisy were both selling ads and doing a great job of it. However, we soon lost both of them. Mary decided to go back to school right around the time that Daisy gave notice. So we placed an ad in the newspaper. This brought us a truly international group of new applicants: Aquinas Gamin, from Sri Lanka, Tony Kenny, who had just stepped off the plane from Ireland, and Joanna Johnson from Ghana, Africa. All had legal working papers, and they became our ad sales and distribution staff for a while.

Jerry's partner Bill was getting close to death at this point and was in and out of the hospital on a regular basis. Jerry worked in the office only a few hours a week and was understandably quite depressed when he came around. This brought a weird schizophrenic atmosphere to our offices. When Jerry was there, it was usually respectful, quiet, and focused, but when he was away, the office was a loud madhouse. Richard decided that to keep our spirits high we needed a field trip. There was a Whole Life Expo coming up in Los Angeles. Richard had attended the Expo in the previous year and said that it was fantastic.

In the hopes of selling tons of ads, subscriptions, and back issues, we reserved a booth, rented a big van, and made hotel reservations in L.A. Then we loaded ourselves and our stuff into the van and off we went, with me driving of course. With me were

Matthew, from Southern California; Yuka, from Japan; Bingo, from Detroit; Richard, from St. Louis; Aquinas, from Sri Lanka; Tony, from Ireland; and Joanna, from Africa. We drove down in one long day and checked into our hotel. Matthew, Yuka, Richard, and Joanna shared one room and I shared the other with Tony, Aquinas, and Bingo. How can I possibly describe the three insane days that followed? It was kind of like the Little Rascals meet Jack Kerouac on the road with Ken Kesey's acid tests, all as filmed by Fellini. With an order of culture clash on the side. We didn't sleep much, and we didn't sell many ads, subscriptions, or back issues. We may have made just enough altogether to cover our time, food, gas, lodging, etc. But we did laugh and see Los Angeles as never before or since. It was a wild few days, but it did help build team *esprit de corps* that helped us weather the worsening situation with Jerry's lover.

During Bill's long battle with AIDS, Jerry attempted every type of magic, affirmation, visualization, ritual, health diet, herb, supplement, and prayer that he could think of. He performed them all to the best of his ability over and over and over again. Sadly, Bill had grown so sick by this time that he seemed to have resigned himself to death and nothing could help him.

I have come to believe over the years that magic, spiritual power, ritual, alternative healing, and manifestation cannot always be used to impose a person's will and intent on reality. The more you practice and refine your intent and skills, the more likely you are to bring about the desired results. However, I doubt that any of these areas will ever become an exact science, any more than poetry or painting. I believe that there are countless powerful forces at work in the universe and on our planet. If a magic worker is in direct opposition to the divine design or the plans of other, more powerful spiritual entities, then their magic is most likely to be unsuccessful. In addition, it is sometimes true that a person's healing can only take place in the form of death.

Due to prebirth decisions, a loss of will to live, the feeling that one has fulfilled what they came to this planet to do, or because God sometimes has a bigger plan, people do die, in spite of the efforts of their loved ones. To my mind, Bill was one of those people.

Doctors lose patients daily. That doesn't mean that modern medicine is invalid. However, in Jerry's case, everything that we had printed, believed in, and learned was ineffective in bringing Bill back to health. I think that this destroyed Jerry's willingness to completely believe in *Magical Blend* from that point forward.

That December, after a courageous battle lasting more than two years, Bill died. On his deathbed, he asked Jerry to renounce all of his useless New Age spiritual mumbo jumbo and accept Christ as his only spiritual savior. Jerry promised that he would. I always believed that a big part of who Jerry had been and a large portion of his very soul died that day. He called me from the hospital. I left the office and ran over to the hospital, where I provided support and helped make the funeral arrangements.

Jerry fell apart and entered a phase of confused grieving, which partially consisted of developing a wild social life in the risqué fringe of San Francisco's creative gay community. He came to work most days and did an adequate job. But to me he never seemed quite right again. He told me of his change of spiritual beliefs and that he had returned to Christ as his path and his savior. He didn't feel that it would or should affect his role as copublisher and managing editor. I had my doubts, but Jerry proved me wrong.

I'll always remember Jerry's wonderful "Perspectives" column, which came out in issue #26, shortly after Bill's death. I always felt it was some of Jerry's best writing and one of the best pieces we ever featured in *Magical Blend:*

There's a drugstore not far from where I live. When you go in the store, you pass through a turnstile. It only turns one way, so once you enter the store, you cannot change your mind and turn around and go back out.

There's also another turnstile that lets you out, and it, too, turns only one way. I always walk through the turnstile entering the store without a moment's hesitation, but on exiting, I invariably pause, full of the certainty that I've forgotten something. I'm not talking about a major anxiety attack, but there is a distinct unease. The question is: Why should I feel that unease? It's certainly no great feat to just exit the store, and then go back in through the entrance. I'm not that lazy. Just between you and me, I think my little neurosis has less to do with the toothpaste or razor blades that I forgot to purchase, than it does with what those turnstiles represent to me.

When you think about it, life is pretty much forward motion. We enter into our experiences, fill up our basket with necessities and goodies, pay our debts, and leave. It's no big deal; it's life. We don't give it much thought until the experience is past, and we realize that the turnstile has closed behind us. Then it's not as simple as just reentering the experience. Life's turnstiles are not as forgiving of absent-mindedness as is the drugstore's. Maybe that's where the unease comes in: that insignificant little border crossing at the drugstore tugs at the memory of all those other crossings, and reminds me of their finality. Adolescence seals the boundary to childhood, and adulthood closes the door on youth. When you cannot turn around and walk right back in, what you've forgotten becomes a good deal more important.

Thomas Wolfe was a man of poetry; he wrote, "You can't go home again." I'm a bit more prosaic; I'll settle for, "The drugstore closes at five." Either way, the poignancy is the same, and so is the point: Before you leave the store, make sure you've filled up your shopping cart because life's experiences are not exchangeable; they're one-of-a-kind items.

Interestingly, as I said before, I do not pause at the turnstile going in. I guess when it comes to life's drugstore, I'm an impulse shopper. I've always tried to think of life as an adventure, and I consider that a gift. But every talent has its shortcomings, and the downside of adventurousness is that it is not this step, but the next that dominates consciousness. In the middle of an experience, I have no vision of it: its face is the blur of motion, full of doubt and contradiction. It is only when the experience is over that I realize its wholeness, and I can begin to see in its outline a beginning, a middle, and an end. And though I sincerely try to appreciate the "now" of each experience, I must admit that I'm rarely successful. Generally I'm one step ahead of myself, pretending to revel in the present while secretly plotting the future—looking for aisle B when I'm standing in aisle A. Then, when I get to that damned turnstile, I realize that the present has suddenly become the past. Even so, things generally work out all right. So what if I forgot the toilet paper I went into the store to get? You can always get toilet paper. There are other items—other experiences—that never make it on the shopping list, and sometimes those are the best.

For example, about six years ago I went on an impulse binge that I never stopped long enough to think about until now. As usual, it was all a blur of forward motion until a point of departure put things in perspective. You see, one of life's turnstiles just recently closed behind me. This time, the turnstile was the death of my lover, and, for once, instead of being full of misgivings about the things I may have forgotten, I am appreciative of the beauty of the past, the essence and totality of an experience that only comes when the experience itself has gone.

Bill was definitely an impulse item. I was not shopping for a lover. The fact is I already had one. The partnership

I abandoned was in its twelfth year, and had accompanied me through some major life changes itself, beginning as it did when I was only twenty years old. The breakup of that relationship was very traumatic, and when its turnstile closed on me, I was absolutely immobile with the thoughts of all the things I had forgotten. At the time, I rationalized my decision to end one relationship and enter into another by telling myself that twelve years had established a bond of love with my first partner that would transcend the narrow category of lover. It would take work, but the love would remain. Meanwhile, through a series of illogical choices, another love had entered into my life. That new love required nurturing or it would be lost forever. I caused all three of us a good deal of pain by holding firm to the crazy notion that I had a chance to hold on to the love of two very special people. And, miracle of miracles, that's the way things eventually turned out, but there were a couple of years in which I was haunted by my selfish megalomania.

I remember my first lover asking me what it was that so attracted me to Bill; I replied with some unfeeling comment like, "The sex is good, and I like his childlike quality." What I didn't know at the time was that less than six months later Bill would become preoccupied with the prospect of AIDS. The sex ceased, and his childlike wonder became choked by the terrible grip of a child's fears. Those fears proved to be well-founded when Bill was eventually diagnosed with AIDS.

In retrospect, the ironic thing about all of this was that lust propelled me into a situation in which love completely transcended sexuality. For myself, love and sexual passion never became separated. For five and a half years I was constantly horny, sublimating my passion in everything but sex. Who knows, perhaps this sublimation was instrumental not only in keeping my two distinct loves vibrantly alive, but also in the development of *Magical Blend,* which both partners always accused of being my mistress. And though I don't advocate sexual sublimation as a logical approach to life, it taught me a lot about love I never knew before. One of the things it taught me was that "marriage" is a divine bond that requires neither social sanction nor sexual satisfaction. Sharing the course of a long, destructive illness that ended with a very ugly death was a profound experience that absolutely shattered the notion of conventional "morality." For those moral mavens who find my personal expression of brotherly love disgusting, I can only feel sorry because, to me, that attitude reflects an ignorance of love. They are the people who go into life's drugstore not only with a shopping list, but a shopping list prepared by someone else. They do not pause at the turnstile going in, nor do they reflect on the way out. They go home with the toilet paper they came for, but all the impulse buys that make life an adventure are sadly lacking.

One part of my life is over now, and though I miss it, and mourn its passing, as I pause at the turnstile that has just closed behind me, I feel no pangs of remorse. For once, I don't think I forgot anything. After all, when you come out of the store with a shopping bag loaded with love, who needs toilet paper?

I had always said we didn't care what employees believed as long as they had open minds and were tolerant of other beliefs. Jerry quoted that back to me. Over the next ten years, he never allowed his beliefs to alter what *Magical Blend* was or argue with its eclectic, nonreligious stance. Yet up until 1987, Jerry had a vision of a fruitful and productive future that bred a strong enthusiasm and drive. After that, his future was at best unseen, and he lived from day to day. Although I believe that *Magical Blend* was always important to him, he no longer seemed to think of it as the vehicle that would someday make him a famous elder statesman in the mold of Buckminster Fuller, Gore Vidal, or Houston Smith. This piece Jerry wrote was his beginning attempt to deal with Bill's death.

Live, From San Francisco, It's . . . *Magical Blend*?

In the middle of 1989, we started the *Magical Blend* television program. I had been doing radio and TV interviews whenever the opportunity presented itself since *Magical Blend*'s inception. Earlier in the year, I had appeared on a Bay Area program called "Today's Health." I was interviewed at the same time as a Dr. Kristin Van De Carr, a specialist on prebirth health for mothers and children. Kristin had some amazing beliefs and practices. The interviewer, Amy Aquarian, was wonderful and she played us off each other so well that at the end of the show I felt as if I knew them and the production staff as friends. We all went out and had drinks afterward. A month later, Amy invited Kristin and me back because the response from the viewers had been so great. Again the show was fantastic. Afterward, Amy informed us that she and her husband had just received a great job offer in L.A. She and the producers wanted Kristin and me to take over hosting the show.

Well, what can you say to an offer like that? Of course, we agreed. Every week for the next six months, Kristin and I recorded a live, one-hour episode of "Today's Health." When Deborah and I got married and went on our honeymoon, Kristin did the show on her own. Upon my return, she said that the show had become too much work and she just couldn't do it anymore. I spoke about it with the *Magical Blend* staff and everyone agreed that the publicity from doing the show had been great. We agreed that we would start our very own *Magical Blend* show. Actually, we didn't all agree. Bingo said to count him out and Jerry was supportive but didn't want to be involved. So Richard, Matthew, Yuka, and our old friends Michael Epstein and Jeff Fletcher, along with most of the production crew of "Today's Health," launched the weekly, one-hour "Magical Blend Magazine Show." We recorded sessions live in a studio at first but that was very expensive and inconvenient, so we began doing them in the office. The best shows were the ones when a celebrity or even an interesting advertiser dropped by.

The *Magical Blend* show soon took on a life of its own. We had all kinds of interesting perspectives and strange moments that went out over the airwaves. Michael Epstein on his travels inter-viewed people from all over Europe and Russia. We often featured Jeff, Matthew, and Yuka's weird and wonderful industrial rock group, Cardinal Sin. My big claim to fame was interviewing Caroline Myss before she had a best-seller. That was fun and grat-ifying. Our best ratings, however, were the result of a massive mis-understanding. At the end of one week's show, I told the viewers to be sure to tune in the following week, for I would be interview-ing Lillian Carter about Oakland and human services. People thought I was planning to interview former President Jimmy Carter's mother! Well, the Lillian Carter that I had in mind was actually a sweet African-American woman from Oakland who had marched with Martin Luther King, Jr., and worked with me at Fred Finch. I suppose that the viewers were a bit confused but it turned out to be a great show, anyway.

Parenthood

In April of 1990, Deborah and I became parents when we adopted our children from Peru. As one might expect, this momentous occasion changed our lives forever. Our children, Henry and Sophia, have given us more joy that either of us could have ever hoped for. They have been dreams come true. Unfortunately, the actual process of the adoption itself was some-thing of a nightmare.

Making a family was something that we had expected to do after our marriage. With all of the hungry and unwanted children around the world, we agreed on adoption from a third-world country. After returning from our honeymoon, we began to investigate the best countries from which to adopt children. Eventually, as fate and the Peruvian spiritual forces that affect my life would have it, Peru appeared as our only viable option. That mystical land has always had a special hold on me, from the first time I visited as a college undergraduate. It only seemed right to adopt our children from the place that had helped form my personal vision of sacred spirituality. I have written at length and great detail of my connection to Peru and the adoption of our children in my book, *The Secrets of The Ancient Incas.*

A Peruvian social worker convinced Deborah and me that we would be in and out of the country in three weeks, at most. However, upon arriving, we soon found ourselves trapped in bureaucratic hell. But that wasn't all. There was a civil war going on in Peru at the time, which made everything dangerous and dicey. The day after our arrival, we were in the process of signing the first in a series of endless legal documents to begin the process with Henry. There was a very loud baby in the office. We were told that there was no room for her in the orphanage and could we possibly adopt her as well? The baby was suffering from malnutrition and her eyes didn't respond to my hand waving over them. We weren't sure if she was blind or worse, but Deborah and I looked at her and then each other. We couldn't refuse. We took this baby into our family as well, and named her Sophia. We spent much longer than we thought would be required to make everything official in the middle of a civil war and a national election. Many times we feared for our lives and our sanity. Finally, after spending nearly four months in the country, we became a legal family. The four of us returned joyously from Peru in July of 1990.

We arrived at the L.A. airport after a twelve-hour flight from Peru. Henry did not stop screaming at the top of his lungs the whole way. No one smiled at us when we left the plane. No sooner did we get in line at customs than Deborah began to turn green.

She said, "Michael I am so ill and nauseated that I can hardly stand up. You have to get us through customs." So there I was with a very sick wife and a screaming son and daughter. I did my best explaining our adoption to the customs official. I must have done OK because they barely searched our bags. Soon we were waiting for our plane to Oakland. Henry screamed some more but Deborah started recovering her natural color.

When we landed in Oakland it was as if we were in yet another foreign country. Nothing seemed the same as when we had left almost four months earlier. We took a taxi home. Sophia slept while Henry stared out the window in shock. When we got home, I called the office to announce our arrival and invite everyone over. All the staff and my sisters and Deborah's friends Marie and Lucy all came over to welcome us back and meet the children. Most of them even brought presents for the kids. Everyone was happy that we were home safe at last. The *Magical Blend* crew brought over a copy of issue #28. I hadn't seen it and didn't realize that it had gone out with so few paying ads. But the reunion was tremendous nonetheless.

Everyone fell in love with the kids instantly. We were too exhausted, full of stories, and high on adrenaline to stop. If we did, we probably would have passed out. As the sun set we ordered out for pizzas. Henry and Sophia loved U.S. pizza as soon as they tasted it, and in fact, still do to this day. We all talked and played very late into the night. There were so many stories to share. What a wonderful welcome home after such an intense time in Peru.

The next morning, I drove into the office around ten. The staff had held the magazine together reasonably well, but it was clear that the business part of the equation was in disarray. Jerry had done a valiant job keeping the ball rolling, but he wasn't an ad salesman. All the people on staff with any sales skills had resigned very soon after I left. Besides, I had assured him that we would be gone for only three weeks, not four months.

During my absence, Jerry had hired an assistant named Cat.

Now, Cat lived on the streets of the Tenderloin and was addicted to crack cocaine, but she usually tended to her habit after work and on the weekends. On their own, Jerry and Cat had done a valiant job of attempting to sell ads. They had sold enough to get the issue printed. However, the debt had grown significantly and was again a major concern. Still, everyone was moving forward on issue #29. The issue looked good except for one problem: There were hardly any ad sales. Yet, even in the face of our debt and slow revenue stream, I was confident. So we had a debt! No problem, we had been in worse places before and I was sure that we could get out of it. I was pretty sure that I knew how to do it, too: Hire more talented, driven people to help us work the debt away.

Now, this was the summer of 1990, and no one was talking about the fact that the country had begun to slide into a recession. As a result, my best efforts in the years that followed were to little avail in turning around our financial position. I had no way of knowing then that the debt would grow and haunt me for the next six years of my life.

Later that week, my in-laws arrived to meet their new grandchildren. They were so happy; like everyone else, they fell in love with Henry and Sophia at first sight. Everyone was happy, but I was already starting to feel stretched thin. My business was in financial trouble. I was a brand-new father. I hadn't been apart from my family for more than four months, and now I had to deal with the reality of juggling work and a home life. Plus, I was dealing with my in-laws, who, lovely as they were, added to the stress at that particular moment.

On the third day of their visit, they all decided to drive over the Bay Bridge and visit me at work. They all came into my office in the middle of a hectic day. Henry was crying as usual. I fell apart. "Who am I, a publisher or a father?" I boomed. "I don't know how to be both at the same time! I can't have you here!"

They didn't stay very long. The ride over had been rather intense and their visit had started the same way. I attempted to calm Henry down with no success. They left shortly thereafter, with Henry screaming and my identity shredded into a million pieces. For the next two years I was generally sleep-deprived, confused, disoriented, and exhausted. I developed a disturbing tendency to mumble and walk into walls. One day I was late for work so I tried using the car pool lane over the toll plaza of the Bay Bridge. I got a $275 ticket and freaked out. Two weeks later I went to court and explained about Peru and the adoption and my confusion and the business, etc., etc., etc. The judge was so moved that he let me off with a warning.

A few weeks later, I was trying to finish my "Potentials" column for issue #29. I was holding the issue up; I just couldn't focus on my writing with everything else going on. My wife had to work late that day, so I was home alone with a one-year-old daughter and a two-year-old son. I was attempting to write while I fed and took care of them. I had Sophia in one hand and Henry in the other. Before I knew it, Sophia had dirtied her diaper and Henry had to pee. All at once I had baby shit all over me, and my son was peeing on my papers. They were both crying; I began to cry, too. Then I cleaned them both up. I also cleaned my way through the mess of a column that I had begun. I started again, this time writing about the joys and struggles of parenthood. It was one of my better-received columns.

The Northstate

That Christmas, we had a wonderful staff party at Jerry's San Francisco apartment. We all got together, exchanged presents, celebrated the old year, and looked forward to the new. Then it was decided that we should all walk to the bar at the top of the Mark Hopkins Hotel for a last drink. All 16 of us squeezed together into the elevator in Jerry's apartment building; not surprisingly, we exceeded the weight limit. The elevator went down for a little while without any problem, but then it got stuck between floors. We laughed, but after ten minutes, we still weren't moving.

Eventually, we pried the door open and crawled out one at a time through a three-foot gap at the top to the tenth floor. All of us were dressed in our better clothes. We were certainly a sight to see. In the process, one of the larger members of our staff got stuck and it took us all another ten minutes of heaving and pushing to get her out. We all then hiked down the stairs and out for that drink, wondering at the symbolism of it all.

Thus, 1991 began on a high note, but unfortunately not much changed with the business. I felt that Jerry resented me because I had left him with the magazine for that extended period of time while we went through our unexpected Peruvian adoption delays. The business limped through the next year. We put out quality issues with some great art and editorial, but ad sales were still slow and revenues were not what they needed to be for us to work our way out of debt. I was more than a bit overextended as a new father of two infants as well as publisher and ad manager for *Magical Blend.* Meanwhile, the debt continued to grow through the year.

It's amazing how parenthood changes one's perspective on things. Deborah and I had lived in our home in Oakland, together or apart, for a few years at this point. We always felt comfortable living there. However, we were both clear that raising two small children in a smallish house with a tiny backyard in Oakland's so-called "murder corridor" wasn't such a great idea. So in August of 1991, we made an offer on a small farm outside the town of Chico, in California's rugged Northstate near the Sierra Nevada mountains—about 200 miles from the *Magical Blend* offices in San Francisco. Our offer was quickly accepted. Deborah and I were thrilled. Now all I had to do was figure out a way to tell Jerry and the rest of the staff.

I went to Jerry's apartment on Post Street to deliver the news to him away from the office. I knew that he wouldn't be happy, but it was even worse than I had anticipated. Basically, he went ballistic. "You can't do that!" he cried. "I hate the Northstate! Chico is

over three hours from the city! Are you quitting the magazine or
do you expect me to quit? I'm definitely not moving to Chico! OK,
then—I quit. It's all yours. Take it to Chico with you."

I took a deep breath. "Jerry! Calm down. We can work this out,
I promise. I've been giving this lots of thought over the past few
months. I can spend three days in San Francisco, sleeping at the
office and supervising everything. Then I can spend Thursdays and
Fridays in Chico selling ads from my new home. I can do this for six
months or more. You always wanted to do more supervision—here's
your opportunity. Eventually, when members of the staff leave, I can
open a small branch office up there and hire replacements. If you
want, you can keep the creative offices here in the city. You'll have
an assistant editor and Matthew and Yuka as well. I will have ad sales,
circulation, and administration up there. But I'll continue to come
down either right before or right after each deadline."

"No, Michael—this won't work! I can't believe you're doing
this. This whole thing is all about you doing it all by yourself. After
Bill died, and you got married and adopted your kids, everything
changed. I don't think I believe in what the magazine is about anymore. When Bill was dying, I tried all the techniques, but nothing
worked. Then he began praying to Christ. He begged me to
become Christian again with him. I said I would. He was so far
gone by then that all I could pray for was a good death for him.
We were both scared, but I think he got a good death. Now I hear
him speak to me from heaven. I believe he is with Christ. I just
want to enjoy life for as long as I have left to live, and I'm not sure
that *Magical Blend* is a part of my future. In fact, I'm pretty sure I
don't have a very long future! You're not HIV positive, and you
probably won't die of AIDS. You're building a future for yourself,
your wife, and your children. Now you are buying a farm in the
country. I don't see how we can continue working together. Either
buy me out or find someone else who will buy me out on your
behalf. We have a fairly large debt on our credit cards already, and
I don't think we are good enough businessmen to ever get out of

this debt. Maybe we should both attempt to sell it and then we could go our separate ways and start over. I'm tired of working every day and I just don't care any more."

Jerry's negative attitude really took me aback. I hadn't known that he was that sad and pessimistic. But I wasn't about to give up without a fight. "Jerry, you're a great writer and a fantastic editor," I told him. "You have been my best friend for years. I don't care what you believe in. You can still write and edit with the best of them. Moreover, I don't want to do this without you. We will get out of debt somehow. I don't think that either of us really wants to sell *Magical Blend* or get involved with new partners. Think about what I'm proposing—I know that we can make it work."

After more haggling along these lines, Jerry very reluctantly agreed to give it a go. I knew that he wasn't yet ready to give up on the magazine or our partnership. His agreement paved the way for the next chapter in the evolution in *Magical Blend.*

Our Oakland house sold just a few weeks after we put it on the market. So, on Labor Day 1991, we emptied out our old home with the help of *Magical Blend*'s staff and other good friends. Jerry and my sister Pat, along with several folks from the magazine, accompanied us on the three-hour drive to our new home. We unloaded the vans and our huge, overflowing U-Haul. Then we all drove over to a tiny Middle Eastern restaurant about four miles from our new home. I don't think they had ever had so many customers at the same time, before or since.

Pat and Jerry spent the night to help us settle in. Jerry's mood had changed considerably since our initial, heated conversation in San Francisco a month or two earlier. Now, as we stood outside and cast our eyes around my brand-new farm-to-be, he said, "Michael, I see it now. It's a look I used to see in my father's eyes when he looked out over our farm in Missouri. You have that same look of proud ownership and unrealized potential. It was a good thing you did. I hate this area but I understand now why you moved here, and I wish you the best of luck."

Many things had led me to this place in my life, which had intensified in an upward spiral from birth. My upbringing and formal education had shown me one kind of life, but then my own travels and experiences as a young man opened up an entirely different path. In my first visit to Peru, I felt that the Inca spirits had given me a life assignment to bring lost and little-known spiritual knowledge to the world. Starting *Magical Blend* increased the intensity and enriched my experiences. Jerry's HIV diagnosis had upped the ante. My relationship with Deborah and our subsequent marriage changed everything once again. Of course, adopting Henry and Sophia was a huge event in my life. Talk about embracing your fears—one day no children, and the next, two! Then came the move two hundred miles to the hinterlands of California, with a newly unemployed wife and two very young children. It had been an amazing ride so far, but the magic was still taking on new forms and expanding in yet unforeseen ways.

The year that followed was spent commuting from Chico down to San Francisco on a regular basis. I would drive down on Monday, spend two, three, and sometimes four nights living in the office, and then make the long drive back home to spend the end of the week and the weekends with my family. It was a difficult, grueling time, for me as well as everyone associated with the magazine. We all put forth maximum effort, but still our debt continued to hang around and even grow.

Toward the end of the year, I started to have pain in my lower abdomen. Of course, being so busy with work and the family, I ignored it. Before long, however, the pain had become too severe to ignore. I went to my doctor just before Christmas and discovered that I had a fairly serious double hernia—probably the result of all the moving a few months earlier. I was upset, but determined not to let it ruin our first holidays with the kids. Jerry, along with my sisters, Pat and Nancy, came up to the farm for Christmas. I was not in the best of moods, but it was a great Christmas nonetheless. Their being with us made us feel less isolated.

A couple of days after Christmas I went into the Chico hospital. Two doctors who I hardly knew operated on me and repaired the hernias. I took a few weeks to recover from the surgery, and then I was right back on the road every week. The first half or more of 1992 was hellish. It was quite a challenge to supervise the staff and keep everyone motivated when I was only there three or four days a week. At the same time, Deborah and I were attempting to carve a farm out of five undeveloped acres of weeds. By July, we all needed a vacation, so we took the family back to New England for two weeks. Getting away often lends perspective. During my time away from California, it became clear that I was overdue to open our branch office in Chico. I commuted for two more weeks after our return, then explained my new plan to Jerry. He was none too enthusiastic, but agreed to support me as best he could.

I opened the Chico office shortly thereafter. On most days, I would be there to unlock the door at 8 A.M. I would travel to San Francisco for a day or two near a deadline or when Jerry and I had big business decisions or disagreements to work out. My trips down to the Bay Area generally occurred about once a month, which was far easier on me than my previous schedule. Otherwise, for that first year in our Chico office, I sat in the front of the room with eight desks facing me, nine phones, nine old Mac computers networked to our database, and a fax machine. At its peak during that time, I had about 12 part-time students coming in and making nonstop prospecting calls. I would make calls as well when I wasn't supervising or coordinating other responsibilities.

Meanwhile, in San Francisco, the magazine gave up our much-beloved office above the Golden Gate Theater. It was just too expensive, and we didn't need all that space anymore. Jerry found a much more reasonable place, on Valencia Street in the Mission District. Jerry and his new lover, Randy, moved into the back area, which had a kitchen, a bedroom, and a small living room. The

Magical Blend offices were located in the three large rooms at the front of the place. We moved half of the office furniture and equipment there and then I took the other half, along with our inventory of back issues, up to the Chico office.

Creating the Chico office on my own and from scratch forced me to confront many of my old worries and doubts. Could I set up and run an office? Could I hire, train, and supervise a staff all by myself? Most importantly, could I set it up so that we made money, not lose it? Finding the right people and integrating them into the *Magical Blend* way of doing things took a few months.

Of those people, one will always stick out in my memory and be a close friend. I hired Paulette Bauer just like all the other part-time salespeople, but she immediately outshone most people I had worked with. She took to selling ads fast and well, and soon she was outselling all the others. Then she began volunteering to assist me in organizing the office, training new hires, and anything else that needed doing. (Paulette was in a committed, long-term relationship, and her lover was very much a full-time student.) She had a great deal of free time and energy, and almost immediately fell in love with *Magical Blend*'s vision. I fell in love with her, but on the highest, purely spiritual level.

Paulette had had a difficult youth and was working hard to heal and dedicate herself to her own evolution and helping others. If she hadn't been in the office doing all she did I can't imagine how I would have gotten through the first year of setting up a branch office in Chico.

By the fall of 1992, I had built a well-oiled office and ad sales machine that was working smoothly and making money. I had answered many of my own questions, and things seemed to be getting back on track.

Then I started having stabbing pains in my chest. On a Sunday, while winterizing the farm, it became difficult to ignore. I went to my doctor's office first thing Monday morning and had a series of tests. My heart was as strong as a horse, and my lungs were fine, as well. However, the tests showed that I had a large growth between my heart and my lungs. The doctor was pessimistic—he believed it to be an advanced form of cancer. The next week, I went to a friend's doctor for a second opinion. This doctor also concluded that it was a large, cancerous growth. Next, I went to a specialist, who insisted that I needed an operation as soon as possible. He believed that there was a chance that they could get all of the cancer out, but the odds were against it. It seemed as though I might die either on the operating table or soon thereafter.

I fell apart. Deborah, the kids, the farm, the magazine—how could they possibly go on if I died? I was crying in the office and Paulette ask me to go for a walk. She tried to give me hope and support in her loving way, telling me about a friend of hers named Laverne R. Denyer, who was an extraordinary psychic healer. I made an appointment that very hour and drove 50 miles south to Yuba City in order to have my healing. Laverne was great on so many levels. Most importantly, she gave me hope. She told me that I could stay alive and be healthy again if I really wanted to, yet warned me that I had set up this event before my birth in order to allow me to leave my life before it became really demanding and intense.

It didn't take a thought for me to know that I wasn't done with my life's work. I didn't fear death. But if I had a choice, I decided to stay and do the hard work necessary to achieve my personal and professional goals. Two or three times a week, I made the drive down to see Laverne. Part of me thought that I did have terminal cancer, as three doctors told me, but Lavern transmuted it. At the very least, she helped me deal with my fears and confusion and focused my intent, will, and belief in the areas of healing and recovery. I owed Laverne big time for her priceless help at that point in my life.

Something like that has to change your perspective. It certainly changed mine. I decided that the magazine debt wasn't so terrible after all, and that Jerry had learned something about supervision and management. We were scheduled to send the next issue to the printer on December 14th, then close the offices for three weeks. Therefore, I timed the operation for the 15th—just two weeks before my 40th birthday. I proceeded to ensure that the issue would be the best we had ever done. I sold ads as never before. I made strong editorial decisions. I wrote my "Potentials" column, letting the readers know that it might be my last and why. I took time to play with my kids. I wrote them long letters to read when they were older if I died. I told my wife how much I appreciated and loved her. I counted the leaves on the trees. I savored every sweet minute of life.

The day came for the operation. I can still remember that morning so clearly. I thought that I probably would not come out of it alive. The doctors had warned us that there was a 75 percent chance that I would die on the operating table. If I did live, there was only a 40 percent chance that they would be able to get all of the cancer, and I would have to deal with massive doses of chemotherapy. Deborah accompanied me into the operating room. Her last words to me were, "You have to live!"

I awoke several hours later in excruciating pain, but alive. I gave thanks for that despite the pain. After a while, the surgeon came in and gave me the great news that the growth wasn't cancerous. However, they weren't sure what it was, so they sent samples to the laboratory. My next memories are of lots of morphine and dreams of Peruvian sacrifices. Days later the results came back from the lab. It seemed that mine was a rare case in which my thymus gland, which is supposed to stop growing and begin to atrophy in youth, somehow continued to grow. Eventually, it grew to a huge size in my chest, thus causing my pains. The upshot of it all was that the doctors said that I would be able to live a normal life. (Me? Normal?) Anyway, I would live. That Christmas was one of rejoicing and thanks. On December 30, I turned 40, feeling as though I had been given a new lease on life. What I did with it from there was up to me.

This experience changed me in significant ways. Being near death sure does make you appreciate every moment and every detail of life. We should always live it that way. My younger sister, Elizabeth, and her daughter—my goddaughter Ayla—had flown out from the East Coast before the operation, and unselfishly stayed with us to assist Deborah during my recovery. Were we ever thankful for them. While I recouped, I wrote my next "Potentials" column detailing what had happened and explaining my second chance at life. In the meantime, letters and calls poured in. I heard from old friends that I had lost touch with years before. I also received wonderful letters of support from people I never knew. Years later, I would still hear from readers saying that they were lighting candles in churches and praying for me, while others were performing pagan rituals in the woods. What a blessed life I have lived, to be cared about so much by so many. I hope to be deserving of it all one day.

I healed and was back at work early the next year. Things were much the same business-wise but my perspective was different. While I still loved the magazine dearly and felt the same compulsion to get the material out to the world, I realized that the financial profit or loss associated with *Magical Blend* wasn't everything. I had come to know life and even a little of death; running the magazine wasn't either of them. It was a wonderful lesson to learn.

In 1993, I hired some good full-time people. They eventually convinced me to replace my inefficient part-time student sales program with full-time positions of three or four sales people to constantly be available on the phones and in the office.

In the middle of that year, we made the decision to close the San Francisco office once and for all. Most of our business was now being conducted in Chico, and only Jerry, Randy, Matthew, and Yuka remained in the Bay Area. They all agreed to move to Chico, which meant that we needed bigger offices once again. Our great friend and mailman Rupe found us a deserted but wonderful second floor office right in the heart of downtown on

Broadway. It was just perfect for our needs, and we were able to sign a very reasonable lease. By the end of the year, the team was all back together once again. We were ready to take on the next stage of *Magical Blend*'s evolution, wherever that would take us.

What's Important

All too often in business, as in life, we get caught up in things that aren't important. We spend our precious resources, energy, money, and time chasing the material things that we think will lead to happiness or make us appear successful to others. But what matters most isn't a thing that you can chase, or even touch. Honor, respect, purpose, and love are what's really important. These years showed me that in a big way.

I often think that *Magical Blend* and I came of age simultaneously. At the beginning, we were both brash and loud. Maybe we were a bit overconfident. As the years went by, we smoothed out the rough edges. We matured. By the time I reached the age of 40, after starting the business, nearly losing it, finding my soul mate, nearly losing her, embracing my life, and nearly losing it—after all this time, and all these events, I came to realize that the magazine and I weren't naive kids anymore. We had some life experiences under our belt. Those experiences made me a better person, and I believe that they made *Magical Blend* a better magazine as well.

I have had many fascinating experiences during *Magical Blend*'s evolution. Running a spiritual business with no backing and no business experience is demanding. Running it with heart and with the intention of improving the world is a challenge in the best of economic conditions. Recessions and wars—or even expensive mistakes—can set you back or almost end your existence. Yet you can't get caught up in all that. You must always keep in mind what's important for your business and the people that you work with.

Thus enter intuition, persistence, vision, and magic. It is a tricky juggling act; however, *Magical Blend*'s history shows that it can be done. Over the years, I've experimented with many management styles and many organizational paradigms. Some sound great in theory but just don't work, while others sound harsh but are necessary to keep the organization moving forward in a productive and balanced way. Good hiring requires lots of intuition, and luck as well. I learned to ask questions about past experiences and future goals, how well prospective employees work with a team, and how adaptable they are. Training them very well is extremely important, too. Make sure they are clear on their goals and talk to them about how they are achieving them on a regular basis. However, it's a fine line between giving someone too little training and too much. Over training is very expensive and stifles individual initiative, while under training can lead to many costly mistakes and early burnout.

The best insights I've gleaned about running a spiritual business can be boiled down to these few rules, which I try to practice every day:

1. As in life, clarify your goals.

2. As the boss, take time to visualize and set the energies.

3. Hire people who believe in what you are doing as well as have the skills to do it. Enthusiasm is great but can only go so far, and even the most talented people create imbalance if they are cynical or indifferent about the overall project.

4. Be generous in spirit but frugal in spending. Every penny not spent is two you don't have to earn.

5. Don't keep anyone on staff who is not producing or who has lost interest or drive. It doesn't serve the employee or the company to ignore it when someone's time is past. Thank them very sincerely, and move them along in their own personal evolution.

6. Keep your finger on the pulse of your buyers or consumers. Service is a karmic principle as well as smart business practice.

7. Ideally, give the people what they want just as they want it. When you cultivate a conscious readership or customer base, they will teach you as much as you will teach them.

8. Be willing to experiment and take chances, but start small so that any mistakes are not too costly.

9. Do spells and rituals to bring in the proper spiritual guidance.

10. Always remember why you are in business to begin with.

These concepts have helped me keep my vision aligned on the future, in good times as well as bad. I've benefited greatly from keeping them in mind, and I believe that they've served the magazine well, too. Even after all the changes that we've gone through, *Magical Blend* has retained its core ideals and mission. It's something that everyone associated with the magazine today is very proud of. And that, my friends, is what's important most of all.

EIGHT

THE MATURE YEARS—ISSUES 43–94 (1994–2004)

Staffs Evolve

Lately, we've light-heartedly come to use the term "Blender" to describe anyone who gets our vision of reality. Throughout the years, we've been blessed to have access to an amazing selection of Blenders as staff members. In the early days, many were volunteers, who spent their time thinking about *Magical Blend* and ways to reach people because they loved what we were trying to do. Many of these folks had amazing skills. I still look back at early issues in amazement at the sheer creative genius caught on those pages.

Later, the staffs were just as passionate, yet more professional. The drug and alcohol use dwindled off and eventually ceased. By the mid 1990s, people like Jerry Snider, Matthew Courtway, Yuka Hirota, Richard Daab, and I had been involved with *Magical Blend* for the better part of a decade or more. We had been through the ups and downs. We were veterans, and we knew what message we wanted the magazine to express.

Thankfully, then, we left San Francisco, moved to Chico, and brought in a whole new group of Blenders to help us in our continued evolution. In our last few years in San Francisco, the magazine had gotten a bit predictable. We were interviewing lots of the same people, using some of the same designs, and saying many of the same things. Our readers were devoted but maybe a bit jaded. Through the 1990s, we faced realities that were alternately despairing and hopeful. Yet we were always blessed to find good people who went above and beyond the call of duty to get the magazine to our readers. The staffs changed, but the vision never did.

At the start of 1994, we closed the San Francisco office. Jerry and Randy rented a house in the bordering town of Paradise, while Matthew and Yuka rented a house right in Chico. *Magical Blend* was settled into the rather roomy second floor office on Broadway that we still occupy. I had kept busy in the time just before and after my chest operation, bringing in new people and designing systems that might help us make more money and pay down our debt. We put out some interesting and good-selling issues, but any money we made quickly evaporated. At the end of 1994, *Magical Blend*'s debt was larger than ever before by far. I tried not to think about it, but it was like a guillotine hanging over my head on a daily basis. That debt chased me to bed each night and woke up with me every morning.

Spiritual Supervision

As I write this chapter, DNA just came by the office. It's always nice to see him, but hard for me to believe that it has been ten years since we first met. He was up there in the annals as one of my most unique, interesting, and difficult staff members. DNA was born and raised in New Jersey by an Orthodox Jewish family. They sent him to a strictly Orthodox school. One day in his youth he discovered *Magical Blend* and we became his guidebook into alternative realities. His parents died while he was in college. DNA took his share of the inheritance and followed the Grateful Dead for a few years. He left the tour one day with his Canadian hippie girlfriend and settled down in Chico. He had lived in town for a few years producing free concerts and printing a sporadic newspaper called *The Ball's Edge*. Around the time that I opened the office in Chico, I met him at a local health fair, where we had set up a booth. DNA was performing a standup comedy routine at the same event. After his set, he walked over to our booth, introduced himself, and thanked me personally for providing the magazine that was so important in his development. He tried to talk his girlfriend into applying for a job with us, but she just didn't want to work anywhere. So DNA took a job with us instead. I liked him immediately—he was unique, original, and enthusiastic. He started out selling ads for us ten hours a week. He did great! I increased his hours and he continued to do a great job for the magazine, first in sales and later in a number of different roles.

In January of 1995, I signed us up for the military retraining program once again. We had good luck with this program several years earlier, when it brought the very competent Bingo to our door. This time, I interviewed several interesting-looking candidates. Of those, I picked Talard Miller, a married man with three young daughters, and Ruby Warner, who had fought on the ground during Operation Desert Storm. During a time when I couldn't sell a single ad for two months, she was shooting cannons in the desert. I asked in the interview how she handled stress. She laughed. "I don't do stress. I fought in a war. Stress rolls off me like water off a duck." I wanted to learn this skill. Talard had been mostly stationed in Germany for 12 years in the army's secret service. He knew secrets about UFOs and remote viewing that I still can't write about.

Talard and Ruby were both a bit conservative for my tastes. If I was going to make them my chief administrative assistants, I knew that I would need someone to serve as a spiritual counter-weight. I offered a promotion to DNA. He didn't really want to work full time. He put on Thursday night concerts in Chico's little downtown park and had a million other big and small projects going on. But he couldn't refuse the opportunity to learn to run an operation like *Magical Blend*. Around that time I hired Mike Gorman, a sophomore at Chico State University who also happened to be a computer wizard, to do data entry and maintain our systems. We also brought in the extremely capable and important Kathy Hawthorne as our new office manager. That year, we took *Magical Blend* off CompuServe and Mike created our own website. We pushed circulation in every way possible. I felt that if we poured money into quality growth and quality personnel, we could greatly increase our revenues and pay down the debt. Thanks to the great skills of the people we brought in, we created more income in 1995 than in any other year in *Magical Blend*'s history up until that time. However, our expenses were even higher than our revenues, so we went deeper into debt.

Meanwhile, back to Ruby and her claim that she didn't do stress. Well, it was the truth—Ruby didn't do stress. She barely did life. The Army had taught her not to do anything above the bare minimum needed to survive. Ruby had few insights or ideas, and little enthusiasm for *Magical Blend*. She often came in hung over. Ruby did do late night drinking and carousing but not much else. Since the government was paying her, we gave her every opportunity to perform better. I tried all of my little tricks to excite her about the job possibilities. But when she started falling asleep at her desk, I had had it. I called the man in charge of the veterans program. He was sympathetic, and asked if the three of us could meet together at his office. I explained the problems we were having. He told Ruby that if she wanted to keep the job, she would really have to start working at it. She assured us that she would. Two weeks later, however, we were back in his office, where he helped me fire her.

My style of spiritual supervision has always revolved around letting people be who they are, and then attempting to fit their unique skills into systems that work best for the group. It can't always be done. I feel sorry for people like Ruby, who just show up for life and bring nothing with them. Fortunately, that wasn't true of the rest of our Chico staff at that time. Most everyone was enthusiastic, excited, insightful, and expansive. It was my dream that eventually Talard, DNA, and Kathy would operate the office while I spent time writing and doing public relations.

Perfect Days

Life in the Northstate was sometimes too laid back for me and the other magical refugees from the Bay Area. Yet there were days that bordered on perfection. In March 1995, I threw a Spring Equinox party for the staff at my home. The weather was simply wonderful, and so was the company. The staff all came and brought their friends and families. My lovely wife, Deborah, was a wonderful hostess, and Henry and Sophia were in seventh heaven having everyone at their house. We spent the day swimming in the pool, playing badminton and croquet, pitching horseshoes, drinking beer and wine (the adults, that is), discussing the magazine, and comparing the spiritual differences between Carlos Castaneda and Alistair Crowley. Then we had a feast; afterward, DNA did magic tricks, much to the delight of the kids.

In those days, we had too many bunnies. My kids had gotten a pair of rabbits the previous Easter and we had been giving away bunnies ever since. Eventually we figured out that our lives were made much simpler by keeping the males and females apart. Anyway, we had an Easter egg hunt and then Henry and Sophia brought out the baby bunnies to show everyone. They managed to convince people to take them off our hands. Talard's daughters fell in love with two of them and took them home. They kept them in their apartment for years and treated them as dogs. They fed them well and they became huge.

That day was idyllic, with no arguments and plenty of laughter. We all felt like a large extended family. People had shown up before noon, and by 11 P.M., Jerry and Randy were the last ones left. They just kept drinking and talking about silly stuff. Finally at midnight I said, "Gee guys, you'd better drive home carefully because I'm going to bed."

Sorcerers and Sorcery

We had been publishing writings by the well-known nagual sorceress Merilyn Tunneshende for a number of issues in the mid-1990s. A lawyer for Clear Green and Toltec Artists, Carlos Castaneda's businesses, had sent us a letter threatening to sue us if we didn't print a retraction of one article in particular. This article contained what they perceived as a character assault upon Carlos. Some of his sorcerer lieutenants of the time had let it be known that they were not happy with *Magical Blend* and might undertake a sorcery attack as well as a legal one. Merilyn didn't seem to care. In fact, she wanted us to print an even more inflammatory attack. I informed her that we were leaving her out of the upcoming issue and printing an apology on the letters page. Now Merilyn was angry with us, too. We had never even met this woman, and she had placed *Magical Blend* in the middle of her sorceries with Castaneda. I informed her that we would not be printing any more of her articles unless we were able to meet in person. She laughed and said, "Well, maybe one day I'll show up as a pizza delivery person and then let you know that was me the next week." I didn't laugh. I told her that we had to spend some time with her to be sure that we were allied with a reasonable person who was what she said she was. She needed time to think about it and said she would call me in a few days. Instead, she called back early the next morning and she asked if she could come to Chico and spend the day with us. Two weeks later, she arrived for another doozy of a *Magical Blend* affair.

In truth, Merilyn's articles weren't really that bad. She only partially criticized Castaneda's teachings, but that was enough to get his entire organization up in arms. Now, we were quite divided in our take on the situation. Half of our staff didn't believe in Merilyn's powers, but the other half did. Half were afraid of Castaneda, while the other half thought it important that we continue to print Merilyn.

On the day of her arrival, we all went to my farm for a quiet, relaxed luncheon. I also invited a number of our long-term freelance writers. We spent another lovely spring day in my backyard. Merilyn patiently answered questions from more than twenty staff members and writers from 9 A.M. to 4 P.M. I served beer with lunch. One of the staff members who didn't believe in Merilyn got drunk and called me aside. "Michael, she is talking to me differently while she's talking to everyone else. I hear her in my head. She is telling me to help her and to sell more ads, too. She says if I don't do both my penis will fall off and I will howl at the moon! I'm leaving! She's real and I don't like her. She scares me."

He left and the rest of the day went smoothly. Later, Merilyn instructed me how to cast effective more powerful spells of protection from Castaneda's people and any other spell casters with ill intent. I have used them often and effectively and even learned how to improve on them. Merilyn still writes for us on occasion. The ad salesperson who felt so uncomfortable in her presence sold lots of ads for a year and even helped Merilyn get her first book deal. Then one day, he just quit. I have heard that his sex life is not so good anymore and that he howls a lot.

That wasn't the end of the Merilyn-Castaneda story, however. Merilyn's one-time assistant—let's call her Rachel—has a recurring role in this part of the tale. She had been a friend of Mark Cummings, a brilliant, well-connected scientist and inventor who claimed to have created an effective free energy machine that was destroyed by the CIA. Richard Daab invited them both to my house, to meet Merilyn. Rachel was inspired to go off and study with don Miguel Ruiz, but she quickly became convinced that don Miguel was in league with an evil God of the dark mirror of the

Toltecs, so she left his study group and assisted his son Tres in forming an alternative group in Berkeley. Tres, having a parting of the ways with his father, fled to India. Rachel contacted Merilyn and arranged for her to teach the Berkeley shamanic study group by phone and eventually became her assistant. After a short time, Rachel and Merilyn also went their separate ways. Rachel then met and fell in love with Don Asaper, a native Mexican, who claimed to have worked for the Mafia and the CIA in his Toltec quest to set his people free from U.S. domination. He claimed his direct ancestors were powerful pre-Spanish naguals and magic workers.

Rachel convinced me to interview Don Asaper, but it had to be at midnight by the dark of the new moon. I agreed because he offered to share powerful secrets that would assist *Magical Blend* in bringing about the Golden Age that I so often dreamed of. At midnight, we arranged for him to phone me at my home so that the call couldn't be traced. At first he spoke about things on the surface, in very general terms. But before long, he turned on the recruitment charm and almost succeeded in convincing me against my will to put his picture on the cover. He wanted us to help him become the new Castaneda for the good of the Mexican people. If I had felt that he was sincere and I wanted to believe in him, then that line of reasoning would have surely recruited me. However, it was quite clear to me that helping the downtrodden was not his true goal; rather, he desired fame and the wealth and power that might follow for his own selfish purposes. Finally, I was able to break his charismatic grasp by reminding myself of Castaneda's failings. I quietly cast some protective spells and I began to ask several piercing questions: How could I help to co-create a Golden Age? What results did he have to show for his efforts so far? What was involved in his dealings with the CIA and the Mafia? What positive Toltec magic could he share with our readers that would prove his knowledge and skills?

Don Asaper freaked out once he realized that his spell of entrancement had been deflected. He tried again to say smooth meaningless words to capture me. When I demanded specifics and wouldn't commit to putting the article in print (much less him on the cover), I felt a dark and hurtful energy come into my body. I felt pain, doubt, sadness, and fear of failure. I knew that this bad energy was coming from Don Asaper, so I radiated love and laughter toward it. I felt it leave my body but not my home. I sent a spell after it but it was slippery.

He signed off by saying, "Print a great feature interview soon or you and those closest to you will regret it." Of course, those words just guaranteed that he would never be printed in our magazines. When I hung up the phone, I ran about the house until I felt the dark energy in Henry's room. I did a banishment spell and saw it blast skyward and away. Still, I was concerned for my son. I did healing protection spells and prayers for hours, but for the next two months he had behavior problems and a series of accidents—all minor. I was relieved when this all ended but things could have been much worse. I told Merilyn and Rachel that I wanted nothing more to do with Don Asaper. Eventually, my son returned to normal. The last I heard, Rachel had left Don Asaper and was teaching her own sorcery classes somewhere. I wonder when her Toltec magic connection will come clean and heal right. I pray for her.

Around that time, I began receiving strange letters from a man claiming to be a time-trapped nagual healer from a bizarre future. He claimed that he had helped Castaneda move through time, but because some of the Castaneda minions perceived him as a threat, he was trapped and given a series of psychological handicaps. This man said that he had contacted Rachel from an ad to learn Toltec magic, but that she and Don Asaper had drained his radiant future nagual energy reserve and enslaved him. Eventually, he regained some of his sanity and his energies and escaped their grasp. He attempted to undermine their operation by fighting them in public, but Don Asaper's cosorcerers came up from Mexico and overpowered him. They set a trap for him at a hardware store, where he barely escaped a sentinel whirlwind. When he sensed that another, stronger whirlwind was waiting for him at the nearby Home Depot, he departed for parts unknown. There was something beyond crazy in his letters. I wrote him, telling him that I was sorry that I couldn't help him, but that I very much wanted his assistance in growing my power in dream time. I meditated on this before bed for a week. Not long after, he wrote back, saying that my dream self and my waking self had been purposely separated for now and he couldn't speed up my planned agency of enlightenment.

However, somehow our correspondence had helped him heal his psychological conditions. Even though he was trapped forever in our current time, he was once again completely sane and living with two female sorcerers. He was in the process of writing a tell-all nagual/beyond Castaneda novel, which he promised to send me once completed. Not quite a year later his former wife wrote me to say that he had suffered a sudden and unexpected heart attack in his sleep and he died. I can't help but wonder what really happened to him.

It seems Merilyn Tunneshende and *Magical Blend* and myself have some karma because we keep having intense experiences. One Merilyn story worth retelling took place when I signed an agreement with the Prophets Conference owners. They had held two conferences and were just beginning to establish their reputation. We agreed we would lend our name as main sponsor for their third event in Phoenix. We agreed that we would let them use our entire mailing list, hook them up with our authors, and give them advertising in return for me being the cohost moderator for most of the panel discussions, and us having a booth at their Phoenix event. We were in debt, so it was agreed I would fly to Phoenix alone, would get a rental car and a hotel room, and shoulder the responsibilities of the booth.

We held up our portion of the bargain and the Prophets Conference promoted the event in such a way that many people perceived that *Magical Blend* was solely putting on the event. People had been waiting for almost two decades for us to do such a thing. The event was a sellout. People flew in from Europe, Japan, Australia, South America, and lots from San Francisco. I was given a booth in the back where people came and found us and testified to how *Magical Blend* had touched their lives. There were many great speakers, most of whom we had published in *Magical Blend* over the years.

The Prophets Conference had done well by getting many native American Indian elders and healers to agree to appear for a unique opportunity to speak to Anglos about their people's predictions of doom and gloom. Peter Gorman, the then-managing editor of *High Times* magazine and an ayahusca Peruvian tour leader, was there with his friend and *Magical Blend* contributor Alan Shoemaker and their breathtakingly beautiful (physically and spiritually) Peruvian wives. Peter came to ask my advice how to handle his booth—he had never done one before or since. We hit it off at once. He is a brilliant man and a true radical revolutionary.

I led many panels. Having Robert Anton Wilson and Marilyn Tunnesende debate was great and I knew how to play them to bring out their best beliefs and ways of presenting them. Peter and Oceana, a wonderful Native elder, insisted we say Shawomen instead of Shaman. She introduced me to the group of Native elders as "OK for a white boy."

The first night after introducing Peter Gorman and Alan and their wives to Merilyn and her assistant we all shared some ayahusca. I just took a little and enjoyed a pleasant evening. Merilyn and her assistant took lots and Merilyn began howling in foreign languages, and her assistant, Rachel, went into a very dark hole. She kept crying, "Help me! I am changing into a praying mantis and you have all become black and white two-dimensional cartoons. I won't live in this meaningless world of sad cartoons and no color. You can't trick me, Kusacotalta, nor you, Toltec, dark mirror god of the smoky glass. I escaped Miguel Ruiz and his deals of sacrificing innocence for fame and glory and I will not be trapped. I am too strong to be unimportant or marginalized. Help me, Merilyn, someone, anyone."

Merilyn and Alan kept attempting to calm her down and reassure her, but she didn't seem to be able to hear them. Merilyn, Peter, and Alan and their wives were all different in how they dealt with Rachel, the praying mantis lady. The ayahusca in my system seemed to give me the ability I usually lack to slow down and become aware of all the minute subtleties of people and how they move and speak and what they say with their body language and the energies they give off. For this little window of an evening, I had this perception like a sixth sense and understood many of the levels beyond words and actions where I always live and move faster and faster.

I saw that the two Peruvian women knew death and suffering and were able to trust in life's outworking. They knew through their many losses that each moment of life was to be savored, each personal interaction to be given all their best. They moved smoothly, quietly, and sensually to reassure everyone with their presence and their genuine caring that all was better than fine, and that the freaked-out woman would be better for her dark nightmares.

Alan had some anger and resentment. His help was centered on ending an uncomfortable waste of what should have been a heavenly sharing. Peter has a rare sense of the ironic and was working on evolving himself from a New York editor/writer into a Casablanca renegade hero like Humphrey Bogart, with a deep desire to embrace his wife's lust and joy of real life rather than New York East Coast cynicism.

Merilyn was barely able to stay with us or keep her spirit in her body. When she was mostly present, she would either add something amazingly effective and miraculously healing, or as inappropriate as I could imagine. Merilyn seemed caught up in a dance with many other dimensions and many possible realities and she knew everything was of precise importance, every action mattered, yet she also couldn't care less about anyone or even existence and also knew nothing mattered a bit and any mistake could be corrected eventually. This made her as difficult as her assistant, yet less worrisome. Eventually, Rachel passed out and we all went back to our hotel rooms for a few hours sleep.

The next morning, I monitored a panel discussion on the future. The participants ran the whole range in orating skills. Yet the divide for the audience was between those who spoke sincerely from their hearts and those who didn't. Father John was a native American Indian elder and his speech was rough, but he spoke of terrors of the past for his people and the possibilities of hope in spite of the Native people's dire prophecies for humanity. He reduced us all to tears.

Then Joan Ocean spoke of the messages of love and hope sent here by the dolphins. She too reduced the audience to tears. Then there was Ociana; she made us laugh and cry. Other speakers were much more analytical and dry. They shared good information, yet the audience was not captured because they didn't share their hearts.

Later I monitored a debate with Drunvalo Melchesideck's famous teacher, Joan Ocean, two elders, and a weak New Age teacher. It was a juggle but it came off wonderfully. After each panel, people stopped me and said how wonderful the debaters were and what an amazing job I had done bringing out the best in every speaker.

The second night, exhausted and punch drunk with all of these intense experiences, I was off again on another challenging adventure. Two women, Gloria and Janine, invited me to accompany them in the ritual calling of space ships. We stopped and picked up a six-pack of beer, and each nervously drank two on the way to the ritual. When we got there, the ritual seemed the most ungrounded and unsubstantive New Age performance I could imagine and many people were trying so sincerely to get into it. They wanted it to be real magic, to actually bring in a UFO.

Many sightings had made headlines one year before over Phoenix. I knew there were rituals and ways to call spaceships and I knew these people doing this were nothing but dreamers and wishers, not true achievers or magicians who could mold reality to their wills. I started making suggestions, until the leader asked me to stop. We wished them well and returned to our hotel.

The third day, a fringe extremist group of Christian Fundamentalists decided that the New Age Conference was the devil's plan to confuse their followers, and they called in death threats to all the local media. So the people running the Prophets Conference hired a multitude of military-like bodyguards for all the threatened speakers. This served to make the speakers less available and the audience rather paranoid. People kept coming to our booth and complaining and wanting refunds. They would hardly believe that we just sponsored it and were not in charge.

The conference ended that night and I flew home to Chico. Other than a few bumps and small misunderstandings, the Phoenix Prophets Conference was an overwhelming wonderful experience for almost everyone who attended. I am still honored that *Magical Blend* magazine was involved in assisting the Prophets Conferences in their early development. They have since evolved into a premier organization renowned for conferences now held worldwide where audiences can hear firsthand cutting-edge speakers and transformative information.

We can't leave the subject of nagual shamanic teachers without mentioning Victor Sanchez. We have had Victor in *Magical Blend* often. He grew up poor in Mexico City. He scratched his way in to college and received a masters in anthropology. He was able to meet with Castaneda when he was in Mexico. He went on to study with the Huichol people of northern Mexico. When he went to ask permission in a very isolated village to study them, the village shaman said, "No you can't study us, you have really come to become one of us." Victor lived with them for three years. I have spent time studying with Victor and we have shared many intimate conversations. I feel his teachings are some of the cleanest, clearest nagual teachings available to the general public. To me he is what Castaneda might have been if he had chosen the path of teaching with heart.

Wow! To think that many people have never had the chance to meet a nagual witch or sorcerer. How and why did I choose this life—or did it choose me? In any event, it is wonderful to get these stories into print, even though most won't believe them. Others will cry out that this is the work of demons or the devil. That is how it should be. Few are able to benefit or take power or develop skills. When I first read Castaneda as a student in the 1960s, he showed me that there were ways of thinking and viewing reality that went beyond Western economics, politics, and history. Castaneda espoused the belief that the pre-European, pre-Christian people had seen, known, and moved through a world very different than that of their Western brothers. Many valid aspects of a rich and full universe were available to anyone who broke out of the Western world's spell of enchantment, entrancement, and enslavement.

Castaneda's writings allowed me to create a much fuller life and to learn how to move into alternative realities on rare occasions. I learned to use those experiences to alter my personal universe to conform more to my wishes. There are other ways to do this, like making lots of money or getting elected to political office, but these do not offer the same level of integrity or fulfillment as non-Western sorcery and true magic powered by belief and imagination.

When I finally got to meet Castaneda, it was too late. My hero had been enslaved by his own greedy sorcery. His assistants from Clear Green were using his name to sell what many believe were just traditional Asian, Tai Chi-like theories, and passing it off as an esoteric nagual concept that they called "tensegrity." They had him under a spell of confusion. He was old and sickly and they would only bring him on stage at seminars when they had to. His people hated Merilyn and didn't like Victor Sanchez or Ken Eagle Feather, either. They had sued Victor and threatened to sue Ken. Both were Toltec nagual sorcerers who had appeared in *Magical Blend* and had become my friends and associates. The Clear Green people didn't even like don Miguel Ruiz! It seemed that their goal was to start a new religion called Toltec Tensegrity, with Carlos as Pope and his books as the only approved gospel. To release his first tensegrity video, Carlos agreed to let me interview him. However, his people then demanded complete say over what and who else would appear in the same issue and how it would be laid out. I got up my nerve and said, "No, we very much want an exclusive interview with Mr. Castaneda, however we give no one censorship rights in our magazine." They would not compromise. Instead, someone in the organization wrote an article, which read like a two-page ad for tensegrity, and signed it Carlos Castaneda. Then they got *New Age Journal* to agree that they would lay it out without ads or art and run no other shaman or nagual ads, articles, or interviews in the issue. We missed running the last Castaneda interview but we kept our integrity intact.

When Carlos died in 1998, the *London Times* asked Douglas Rushkoff to write his obituary. He told them that he knew little of Carlos and recommended me. Of course, I was honored to write it. So, in some ways, I had the last word in that sorcery struggle.

Magical Book Publishing

For years we had wanted to publish a *Best of Magical Blend Magazine* in book form, but we knew nothing about book publishing and didn't want to do it ourselves. We had heard rumors that the now-defunct *Mondo 2000,* led by RU Sirius, had received a $75,000 advance from HarperSanFrancisco to print what I thought was a terrible *Best of Mondo 2000.* It ended up selling poorly, which was the final straw as far as I was concerned. If they could do it badly and still get paid all that money, we could certainly do it better.

DNA was being phased out of advertising because he was tired of it and wasn't doing so well anymore. He had decided he didn't want to be responsible for assisting in leading the magazine either. Yet he was so creative that I was desperately trying to find a new role for him. We decided that he would work with me in putting together a book proposal for a *Best of Magical Blend* book that would cover our first fifty issues. He would then attempt to get us a big advance from one of the large book publishing houses. He eventually got a proposal done. It was rough but better than we had ever done before, and he pitched it to every big publisher and agent he could find. We got turned down by everyone! It was that way with most of DNA's projects in those days—none of them were bearing fruit, so we agreed that it was time for him to find other employment. He did and we have remained friends until this day.

A few months after he left, I rewrote the proposal and went to the Chicago American Booksellers Association (ABA) convention (now Booksellers Expo of America, or BEA). I introduced myself to every book publisher I could find and pitched them on our proposal. Most were anything but accommodating. I heard all sorts of objections: "Not our type of thing," "Too unorthodox," "No clearly defined category to put it in," etc., etc., etc.

Finally, after more than two hundred attempts in four days, a small publishing company by the name of Swan Raven Publishers said that they loved our idea but were unable to provide any advance. They were unable to print any of our art and they wanted us to cut our articles almost in half, but they did agree to help us with editing and layout. In exchange for the rights to the book, which they immediately decided to call *A Magical Universe,* they agreed to print and distribute 10,000 copies and pay us a small royalty for each book that sold. We could buy as many as we wanted for only the cost of printing. We were thrilled. It wasn't the big book deal we had dreamed of but it was a book deal. But Swan

Raven soon made the whole process much more difficult when they insisted on our obtaining signed approvals by all the authors, giving us rights to their articles or interviews that we could then edit as we saw fit, and denying the authors royalties or additional compensation. This would be challenging. I returned to Chico with a signed contract in hand and a great deal of additional work to do.

The next week, we received a call from John Nelson, then an editor at Hampton Roads Publishing Company, saying that he had read our proposal and wanted to do our book. (John was the same author who had written us a letter saying he was too busy to write for our first issue.) I told him that they were too late. He hung up, quite disappointed. An hour later, he called back. He had talked to Frank DeMarco, Hampton Roads' chairman, and Bob Friedman, Hampton Roads' president. They had decided that they wanted to do a *Magical Blend* anthology, only they wanted original material by 25 of our most attuned authors, each writing about how people could best deal with upcoming planetary changes. They wanted to call it *Solstice Shift.* The idea was that all the authors would write their piece—or at least begin—on the morning of the summer solstice. We were a bit taken aback by John Nelson's very precise notions of what Hampton Roads wanted, but we agreed to sign a contract. I spent that evening wondering about how we would possibly accomplish these tasks in addition to regularly putting out the magazine. But *Magical Blend* has always had wonderful synchronicities on its side.

The next day, a very talented graduate student working toward his master's degree in English walked into our office, wanting to volunteer as a full-time intern over the summer break. So it was that Tom Reward joined our team. Tom became the main coordinator for doing whatever needed to be done in getting both books completed by August 15. As it turned out, we completed *A Magical Universe,* in time to meet the deadline; *Solstice Shift,* however, ended up taking considerably longer.

As usual, my job was to be the upfront man. I called authors who had written interesting pieces for us in the past to see if they wanted to be included in *A Magical Universe*, along with talented new writers who we might want to use for *Solstice Shift*. Dr. Clarissa Pinkola Estes gave our request deep consideration. Now, while Clarissa was and is one of my all-time favorite writers, she is not one of the easiest or most agreeable authors to work with. Sad to say, she felt that in order to maximize the sales of her own books and protect the sanctity of her message, she had to deny us reprint permission. Jean Houston was equally overextended and concerned, but she managed to come up with a more satisfactory and creative solution in order to get a piece into *A Magical Universe*. She said that we could reprint any piece of hers that we chose as long as she got to do the final reedit on it. Furthermore, she was scheduled to give a lecture on the day of the solstice. If I could get the sponsoring organization to agree to give us the printed rights, she would give the talk with *Solstice Shift* in mind. That was easily signed off on by the organization, so we had Jean Houston committed for both books, which was quite a coup.

Robin Williams's agent approved the reprinting and reediting of his client's interview, but couldn't commit Robin to doing anything new. Lynne Andrews had to call me back after consulting with her guides. When she returned the call, she said her guides loved us! We could reedit her article and she would write a new piece for *Solstice Shift*. Whitley Strieber, who wrote the bestseller *Communion*, loved *Magical Blend*. I consider him and his lovely wife, Anne, personal friends. Whitley also had to get back to me after consulting with his guides or alien friends. When he called back, he said that his advisors liked us and wished us great success on these important books. He gave us permission to reedit his earlier piece. Unfortunately, he couldn't contribute to *Solstice Shift* since it would have a negative effect on his message. So we contacted Barbara Marciniak, another well-known *Magical Blend* UFO connection who had written the bestseller *Earth*. Barbara knew what her reptilian alien guides would say immediately. She and they loved *Magical Blend*, but many people who would be included in our two anthologies would be controlled by the dark forces of the Ananaki Reptilian human shepherds and forced to give misinformation. Therefore, she couldn't participate. Jacques Vallee, another of my favorite UFO authors, said OK to a reprint, and he didn't even have to consult with an alien first. Alberto Villardo, who wrote of Peruvian shamanism, said yes to the reprint, but was too busy traveling to write a new piece. Joan Halifax, who also wrote a great book on the shamans of Peru, did not want to do the reprint but did agree to write a new piece for *Solstice Shift*. Michael Grosso and Marina Ray Booth each agreed to write a new piece but refused the reprint. Similarly, Barbara Hand Clow said she would rather not be reprinted but would love to write a new piece for *Solstice Shift*.

Robert Anton Wilson had become a bit of a curmudgeon by then, and he was still a bit hurt that we stopped using him in every issue. (He had written a regular column for us from issue #15 to issue #35.) However, he had always told people that *Magical Blend* was leading a subtle and quiet but effective revolution, and he recommended reading us for inspiration on a regular basis. He agreed to be in both books. Tim Leary agreed to a reprint, as did John Lilly and Terence McKenna. All three have since died so no one will print original material by them anymore, unfortunately.

Merilyn Tunneshende said she was about to go out to the Yuma desert to perform some intense rituals during a week of fasting, vision questing, and astral traveling, but said she would put our request into the mix and get back to me. I was thrilled when she called two weeks later to inform me that while visiting a dimension peopled by sentient onions who lived in crystalline tunnels, one of them stopped her and said that she should stay aligned with *Magical Blend*. She agreed to participate. James Redfield, who authored *The Celestine Prophecy*, said yes to a reprint and said he would prefer to be interviewed again for a future issue of *Magical Blend* rather than write a fresh piece for us at that time. Dan Millman, whose most famous book, *The Way of the Peaceful Warrior*, inspired a generation, offered to reedit his original article. Douglas Rushkoff, who tells people that we helped to launch his star-studded career, said that he would be honored to be in both books. Ken Carey, whose books are some of the most important ever written (especially *The Third Millennium*), and sadly the least read, said that he was going to stop writing because the royalties didn't pay enough to feed his 13 kids in Missouri. His books were just not reaching their audience and he said that these two books would be two of the last he would do.

David Spangler, who was one of the founders of Findhorn and cocreators of New York's Guardian Angels, as well as the author of many wonderful books, said he would love to be in both books. Unfortunately, Swan Raven left him out of *A Magical Universe* by mistake. The same weird thing happened with P. M. H. Atwater, Peg Jordan, and Robert Stone. All were supposed to be in *A Magical Universe* but due to last-minute editing miscommunications, they only appeared in *Solstice Shift*. Stone has since died, so what he wrote for *Solstice Shift* while living in Cambodia with his wife was his last printed piece. Shakti Gawain felt that her old pieces were too out of date but agreed to be in *Solstice Shift*. Marsha Sinetar thought her piece was too out of date as well and feared that her beliefs and message were too Christian for *Solstice Shift*. I assured her that open-minded Christians such as herself had a responsibility to make their voices, views, and insights heard in our world. She eventually agreed to write a piece on the pagan solstice.

Other big names continued to come on board for one or both projects. Larry Dossey and Andrew Weil, both of whom were published in *Magical Blend* well before becoming national celebrities, agreed to reprints. John Cleese of Monty Python fame wrote us from England, where he was filming a James Bond movie, to say that he couldn't write us a new piece or find time for an interview. He loved *Magical Blend*, but felt that we were too serious, so he advised us to reprint his piece and get a better sense of humor. Jaron Lanier, the man who invented virtual reality, said OK to the reprint. Malidoma Somé said that we needed some ethnic flavor; he approved the reprint and told us to find fresh new ethnic voices to speak for the traditional peoples. Jerry Garcia's people reported that Jerry was sick but said that our interview with him was special and that we should reprint it. Julie Cameron, the Shulgins, David Kyle, Riane Eisler, Stanislav Grof, Natalie Goldberg, Z Budapest, Van Ault's family, and Marlo Morgan each in their own way said that they appreciated *Magical Blend* and would love to have their work included. Out of appreciation for all his hard work, I had invited DNA to contribute a chapter to *Solstice Shift*. I made the same offer to E. J. Gold, who wrote the classic *New American Book of the Dead*. E. J. is without question one of the most thought-provoking, controversial, crazy, and wise characters I have ever known. However, both DNA's and E. J.'s articles came out a bit too tongue-in-cheek. They could have easily been misinterpreted as being cynical and nonempowering, so they were edited out of the final version.

Because of all her help and healing when the doctors had diagnosed me with terminal cancer, and because I was impressed with her original insights into the spiritual aspects of existences, I wanted to include a chapter by Lavern R. Denyer. She had wanted to publish forever but up until then had never gotten her work written properly or edited well. I asked her to record her thoughts about preparing spiritually for the future on the day of the solstice. Tom worked very closely with her to shape it into a great chapter. It turned out to be one of the highlights of *Solstice Shift*. Partially due to being included in *Solstice Shift,* Laverne has now written an in-depth metaphysical book that will be released by a well-known publisher this year.

When we moved our office to Chico, I hired a woman by the name of Sirona Knight to be Jerry's editorial assistant. At the time, she had just written her first book for Llewellyn Publishing. Sirona was a great writer but terrible in an office, so I eventually had to let her go. I was surprised when she informed me that she considered this event not a firing, but merely a change in her job description. Sirona felt that she knew how *Magical Blend* functioned and could therefore write ideal pieces for us. We would pay her for these pieces because we would love them so. At this writing, Sirona has a grand total of 49 books in print and her great writing has been in more issues of *Magical Blend* than anyone other that myself. She wrote a great pagan chapter for *Solstice Shift*. She and her husband, Michael Starwyn, and their son, Skylor, have all become good friends of mine over the years.

The next year, I attended the BEA in Chicago once again because *A Magical Universe* had come out to rave reviews and I was invited to do some book signings. These were pretty heady times. Our first book had been very well received and we were in the final stages of deciding who would be in *Solstice Shift*. While there, I got to meet Ken Eagle Feather. I requested his contribution, but he lovingly said that the energies weren't right for him at that time. At that same BEA, I met Frank DeMarco for the first time. I had read his book *Messenger*, which I loved, as well as the occasional Hampton Roads newsletter he mainly authored and edited. Of course, I requested that he appear in *Solstice Shift*. Frank felt strongly that this was John Nelson's project and, though honored and tempted, he refused. Our meeting was one of those mystical moments because we both felt like we knew each other even though we had never met or spoken. We agreed it must have been past life stuff and that we had karma to work out, because Frank and I have been good friends ever since. His book *Muddy Tracks* is wonderful.

I spent a lot of time at the Hampton Roads booth during that BEA. One day, after a very successful book signing for *A Magical Universe,* I found myself good-naturedly arguing with John Nelson about the details of who should be in the final version of *Solstice Shift.* All of a sudden, a tall and imposing fellow walked over to me and said, "I'm trying to do a book signing over here! You are so loud that I can't hear anyone. Could you please argue else-where, or at least do it more quietly?" We all had a good laugh and he introduced himself as Neale Donald Walsch, the author of a new book called *Conversations with God*. Neale (not quite Neal Powers, but close) thought that *Solstice Shift* sounded interesting. He wanted to contribute a chapter, but John told him it was only for authors who had been in *Magical Blend*. At the same moment, Neale and I said that we should do an interview in the next issue. Neale and I felt very aligned in the work that we were both doing. I mentioned that it would be great to have him more involved in *Magical Blend*. He was curious as to what form that might take. Later that month, while I was interviewing Neale over the phone, he offered to write a column in each issue. I ran down the hall and talked to the staff. We all agreed that if Neale would let us edit his pieces to fit our featured themes, then we would be thrilled to have him in the magazine on a regular basis. Neale wrote an excel-lent ongoing column, which appeared in every one of our issues over the following three years.

After the BEA, the promotions for *A Magical Universe* began in earnest. I had tried to cut a deal with the Ford Group, one of the most renowned New Age PR agencies, but they wanted more money than we could justify. Even though they had represented Dr. Wayne Dyer, Deepak Chopra, and James Redfield, they gave no guarantee and we couldn't risk deeper debt. So we worked closely with Eileen Duhne, Swan Raven's in-house public relations manager. As fate would have it, Eileen was an integral member of Safe Space, the first psychic classes I had taken upon moving to San Francisco. Bill Farr, Safe Space's founder (who had predicted my wife to a "T" years before Deborah and I had met), had died a couple of years earlier, but Susan Sun and a number of the group's other long-term members had kept it alive by performing various rituals and ceremonies. Eileen had worked in Hollywood and had some great insights and connections. She arranged for me to be on television and radio and do book signings and workshops all over the Northwest. She set up national and even international radio and TV show appearances. When *Solstice Shift* was finally released (after John Nelson and I had debated every aspect of it beyond reason), we hired Eileen to undertake a second PR push. She pulled off a repeat performance. The highlight for me was when she arranged for me to do book signings, radio, and TV for two weeks in the Seattle area. I stayed with Richard Daab, who had moved there soon after *Magical Blend* immigrated to Chico. Richard and I spent all of our tiny amount of the free time brainstorming about future editorial and business evolutions. Another PR friend, Jody Winters, did me a huge favor and arranged for me to be interviewed by Art Bell on his all-night radio show "Coast-to-Coast After Dark." I was interviewed from 10 P.M. until 3 A.M.—it went fantastically. However, none of us were prepared for the overwhelming response. When the staff got to the office later that morning, the phone machine was so filled it was no longer accepting messages and all the phones were ringing off the hook. They continued ringing almost nonstop for the next two weeks. We answered phones, took orders, and did little else. We sold lots of books and subscriptions, but we also gave away an excess of free sample copies. So once again, we ended up spending much more money than we brought in and the debt only increased.

One of the Seattle signings was with David Spangler and a very famous wiccan author and tarot designer, R. J. Stewart. So here were the three of us, teaching tarot and discussing the early years of Findhorn and *Magical Blend*, with many of Bill Gates' software geniuses in attendance. Several were like resistant sponges, for once they allowed themselves to believe that we might be sincere and magic might be an arcane yet viable kind of science, they became totally engrossed. We talked as a group until 4 A.M. When I returned to Richard's home, I had received a message that my son was sick. I called up R. J. Stewart for a card reading to determine the cause of Henry's illness. My friend told me that I had been absent from home too long, caught up in my magazine and books. Henry was psychically begging me to be home with him more. That ended the phase of doing extensive PR on the road. I told Eileen that we were done for now, and I let the promotional side of our book and magazine business slide for a while.

As soon as I did that, however, the sales of our books as well as those for *Magical Blend* advertising and subscriptions started to slow noticeably. It was clear that I had spent too much energy and money on the books, in the belief that they would catapult us up to the next level of visibility. They had done that but they had made much less than they had cost and ad sales had suffered terribly. As an act of desperation, I took out an ad in the National Radio Interviewer's guide to guests. We wrote that I was one of the world's foremost experts on UFOs, and since it was almost March, we said that I could speak about how the extraterrestrials have used the IRS and taxes to control humanity. Now, I do believe that the Ananaki created humans from mixing their genes with a now extinct apelike species that was found on this planet. The result of their creation was a slave race meant to supply their planet, Nibiru, with the gold, diamonds, silver, and copper needed to keep it healthy and in its 3,500-year orbit. I further believe that some of these reptilian beings stayed on earth in order to control humans from behind the scenes. In doing so, they created religion, wars, and money to control us and keep us from embracing the godliness that we are destined to achieve. I know that this is far out and I seldom speak of it except to chosen friends. So when I was interviewed about it coast-to-coast, it was rather curious to say the least. I was laughed at and made fun of in every city in the United States. It helped us sell some magazines but was not my most enjoyable experience and not one that I would care to repeat. Even after this somewhat painful final blitzkrieg of PR, we were still sadly wrestling with a growing debt. It had grown much worse and it was obvious at that point that *Magical Blend* would need a miracle to stay in business.

Rising from the Ashes

For a while, having everyone working together in Chico helped heal some of our divisions and opposing viewpoints. However, by 1996, it seemed pretty clear to me that Matthew and Yuka had become very set in having final say in the layout, design, and art decisions and were resistant to taking advice, constructive criticism, or input from me or anyone else. Jerry had become run down from having HIV and taking massive amounts of chemicals to combat the disease; from my perspective, it felt like he had lost much of his interest in keeping *Magical Blend*'s editorial on the cutting edge. He was rehashing old, easy contacts and information. He wasn't doing as much outreach to new writers with fresh perspectives, and he didn't have the energy to make the extra effort to improve our content or make the editorial fresh and unique.

Jerry Snider is still one of the very best writers and editors I have ever met, let alone had the privilege to call friend. His vision, insights, and adaptability—among many other skills—were essential to *Magical Blend*'s unique identity and wide respect in the world. As much as I, Jerry was the heart and soul of *Magical Blend* for the first 19 years. He often fought me to feature articles that he knew our audience would love, even if I hated some of those pieces. Life had been harsh to Jerry, and every business has seasons. He lost his health and enthusiasm just as *Magical Blend* entered a dark, cold winter. We all contributed to the magazine growing stale, redundant, and losing money. In fact, I must take a large share of that responsibility because I was the business manager and advertising sales coordinator.

I realized all of this slowly, and as I was doing so, the debt continued to mount. The magazine's newsstand and subscription sales were slipping quickly and badly. Any new initiatives I tried to undertake to reverse this depressing trend I felt were countermanded or simply ignored because no one saw the need. The morale of the staff and my authority were at an all-time low. No one did much and I felt painfully that we were languishing in mediocrity. It was clear to me that without any cooperation from anywhere else, I couldn't effect the real changes that we so desperately needed to make.

For about the next year and a half, I went through a deep state of depression unlike anything I had experienced before or since. At the start of this period, Talard was still our ad manager, it felt to me that Jerry still didn't care about anything but undermined every action I took, and the business constantly looked like it was sliding toward inevitable bankruptcy. I felt like a total and complete failure. Making matters worse, my wife and I were not getting along (and that's putting it mildly). Deborah was extremely concerned about my huge debt and how a bankruptcy would affect her savings and possessions. Partially due to our constant arguing, our kids were very needy and argumentative as well. I barely enjoyed my family that year, and they didn't much enjoy my company, either. The whole world felt like fingernails on a blackboard.

I would stay in bed as late and often as I could, yell at anyone who came by, and take antidepressant sleeping pills to make it through the night. Eventually, I enrolled in therapy, which lasted about 13 months.

Depression—how does one write about depression? I have been blessed in so many ways during my life. I have always been willing to work hard, adapt and learn whatever I needed to fulfill my goals. Having achieved many things, I was always also blessed with an optimistic outlook. I always wake up excited about a new day of possibilities. I love challenges and view myself as a warrior. No matter what life has handed me, I have been able to transform it to a victory. Yet in my deepest shadow place, even as a very fortunate businessman, I always feared failure. I always feared the dark stamp that bankruptcy would represent. And of course, as I mentioned earlier, I do believe that our obsessions tend to draw the things that we fear the most into the paths of our lives. In retrospect, I believe that we, and I, drew *Magical Blend* into an inevitable collision course with bankruptcy.

At that moment, I hated Jerry, my longtime business partner and best friend. I felt that he wanted us to fail and was doing everything he could to undermine every decision I made toward positive improvements. I offered to buy him out with money I didn't have, but he refused my best offer. He had a good paying job, and as long as I took my pay he got his, and I had convinced myself that he was doing little or no work that contributed to the well-being or continued existence of *Magical Blend*. I resented the hell out of him and had fantasies of sneaking up to his house and killing him and his lover in the middle of the night. They were only fantasies, of course, but they were so unlike me and I kept having them.

My health deteriorated. I got more earaches, viruses, allergies, colds, and fevers that year before the bankruptcy than at any other time in my life. I began to see a counselor. He would listen to me each week and say how sorry he was for me. He and my medical doctor prescribed a series of antidepressant pharmaceuticals for me. None of them seemed to work; most made me tired, anxious, paranoid, or more depressed. Because I was freaked-out, depressed, and angry, my wife became petrified. She began to think that I would stop getting paid, or that I would stop working, or that we would go bankrupt together. She had an irrational fear that some court would take her house, her car, and everything else that she owned, even though we had always kept our financial affairs separate. When it did get so bad that I could no longer take my draw, Deborah went ballistic. We always had a deal that she owned everything but my car and my business, and I paid her money for rent, groceries, utilities, and the kids' needs. Now I couldn't pay my share and she lived in fear and resentment. We argued nonstop. She insisted that I begin applying for jobs. Doing so broke my heart even more. I was offered a couple of good paying jobs in Sacramento at big corporations. I refused them and told my wife that no one wanted to hire me.

One day I fought with myself to get out of bed. I got dressed up better than usual because I felt so depressed. I drove to work, but found myself unable to get out of the car. I just sat there and cried. I was a failure. Everything I had worked to build for the last 17 years was useless. The company couldn't pay its bills. No one wanted to buy it. No one wanted to help us financially. It must be useless. It must be a waste of time. All the good that I thought I was accomplishing for those years, and all the inspiration that I thought I had provided to our readers must have been an illusion. They were just lies I had told myself to keep doing a meaningless job. I had printed over 50 meaningless issues. I just cried and cried and felt like a terrible failure. I couldn't face my staff. I just drove home and went back to bed with my nice clothes on and cried all day long.

Many spiritual traditions have the concept of the dark night of the soul. In certain shamanic teachings, the student must die, travel to the land of the dead, and be reborn, bringing back sacred knowledge that they can receive in no other way. In occult teachings, the wizard in training must step off the cliff fearlessly. He must fall into the blackest pit, losing his very identity, facing and overcoming his deepest fears, doubts, and insecurities. Only then may he emerge from the pit with a new magical identity and truly be a wizard. For me, the bankruptcy and the depression leading up to it represented the dark night of the soul. I became lost in the darkest pit of my fears of failure and ruin. I, who have always been a radiant optimist, was stuck in a pessimistic doomsday scenario.

It seemed for most of that time that no matter what I tried, I could not keep my mind away from focusing on my fears and all that had gone wrong. However, eventually I made myself use the basic spiritual tools and techniques that had worked for me over the years. I prayed daily to the spirit of *Magical Blend*, to Inca goddesses and gods, to many other pantheons, to Gaia, the spirit embodiment of planet Earth, to the universal creative force, to Mohammed, Buddha, Moses, Abraham, Krishna, Kuan Yin,

Hecate, Pan, Jesus, and the Virgin of Guadeloupe. I asked them all to help me find my lost optimism and to visualize an end to my depression and our huge debt. I did rituals attempting to focus my intent and draw magical energies to these desires and hopes. I meditated on the problem, and I chanted whenever possible. Some days were better then others, but a deep depression verging on despair haunted me for approximately a year and a half.

One morning, I awoke to discover that something phenomenal had happened while I slept. My depression was gone. I was still aware of *Magical Blend*'s huge debt and the fact that magazine and ad sales had been in a bad slump for a long time. I still didn't have any solutions or see any way of changing all of that. But I was myself again. I knew that none of my failures and setbacks really mattered worth a hill of beans. No matter what had happen in my life, I had always worked with the circumstances and prospered. This too had just been a challenge, a test necessary for strengthening my spirit. That week I stopped taking antidepressants. I even stopped taking St. John's wort. In two weeks, I finished up with my therapist and from that moment on I was able to deal with life in a new, wiser, and more magical way.

We must see even depression, bankruptcy, and failure as gifts and opportunities. With that and lots of prayers and meditation, things eventually began to change, slowly at first. Then one day the cloud just lifted. Nothing had changed but my attitude, but that was the most important thing.

The staff began to turn over. Talard lost all perspective one day, blew up at me for exploiting him, and quit. That was a shock, because he had been one of my few friends and allies during the previous year. It was a sad loss but I was OK with life again and determined not to slip backwards or falter. We hired a new salesman, Victor Cantu, who was into Bob Dobbs and "slack" and dope and he pushed the balance of the staff's interest and even editorial in those directions. But he was a consistently great salesman and friend who was invaluable to *Magical Blend*'s survival.

Rene Schmidt also came aboard during that period of rebirth. He started as a graphic designer with some amazing skills. His timing was perfect, because Matthew and Yuka soon followed Talard by giving their notice. They had done their best for over a decade, setting a unique and high quality standard for the magazine, but the time for change was upon us all, and we all agreed that they should give their notice.

With all the personnel changes, we began taking concrete steps to refine and save the business. We hired the very smooth Bill Hall to be our new operations director. Jerry liked Bill, so that made the next year tolerable in the office. I developed and maintained a strong resolve to do all I could for *Magical Blend*, enjoy my farm for all it was worth, accept my wife as best I could on her terms, and appreciate my children for the miracles that they were and are.

I have to take time out for an aside to say a few words about the marvelous Rene Schmidt, MB Media's art director and resident techno shaman. It would have been difficult for anyone to follow Matthew and Yuka as art director. They had created countless amazingly artistic and inspired issues. But Rene reinvented the wheel; he developed a unique new style and designs all his own. How does one describe such a creative genius? For me, Rene is best compared to Scotty, Jim Kirk's trusty engineer of the Starship Enterprise. It seems that I am always saying things to him like, "No, we need five pages worth of editorial to fit into three pages of space, along with illustrations and ads and it still needs to invite the readers in and be artistic and readable," or, "No, we don't have the budget for that piece of equipment, even though you need it to help you do the impossible better and faster than ever before." Rene will generally listen to me with a smile and reply something like, "Michael, it can't be done, not in that amount of time with that amount of money!" But then somehow he always does the project better than I dared to hope. He can fix anything that isn't a PC computer (he loves Macs and loathes PCs). He can do marvelous layouts and designs with the most rudimentary of tools. He is even a great writer and editor, yet he fears to admit it, for it might mean more work. He is charming with our advertisers and our contributors. When new employees start with us, thrown into the overwhelming newness and differentness of how our office operates, it is usually Rene who welcomes them, answers their multitude of technical questions, sets up their work-stations and e-mail, and generally makes them feel at home. The list of miracles that Rene pulls off on a daily basis is truly endless, and I never thank him enough. So thank you, Rene.

Back to our story! Much of the stress in my life in 1996 was associated with our company's poor financial position. Most of our debt was with our printers. The lion's share of the remainder was held on credit cards in Jerry's and my names, which we used to cover payroll and buy office supplies when we had no income. The debt kept growing, and eventually it reached, for me, unimaginable heights. Fortunately, Bill Hall came into the company at that time, seemingly offering solutions to all our problems. Now, Bill was very charismatic and he talked a big game. He had lived and worked in Los Angeles and Las Vegas, where he owned, operated, and later sold a magazine by the name of *Nevada Travel*. Bill convinced Jerry and me that we could put together a deal to pay off our debt and expand *Magical Blend*. His enthusiasm and optimism were essential elements to my staying out of depression, along with a session of radical rapid eye movement therapy in Oregon. Even Jerry was reinspired. The three of us began to attack the problems on all fronts.

Not long after Bill started, our new salesman Victor sold an ad to the Marshal Mint, owned by the eccentric millionaire Hugh Roy Marshal. Hugh Roy owned the famous Comstock mine, which had once been in the possession of the Hearst family. At that time, he was producing gold and silver angel coins and medallions. Hugh Roy was very interested in astrology, aromatherapy, the secrets of the keys of Solomon, and most other things involving the New Age. I went to his mansion in Nevada City to meet him. We seemed to hit it off well, despite the fact that he was a successful businessman and I was a struggling, nearly bankrupt publisher. We talked about many things, including his possibly coming in as an investor in the magazine. I went back on another occasion and interviewed him, and he was still interested in lending some financial support to *Magical Blend*. On the next trip, I brought Jerry and Bill. By then, we were all in agreement that Hugh Roy would become our third partner. In fact, he signed a letter of intent and put in a sizeable deposit to prove that he was serious. His deposit money allowed us to print the issue in which his interview appeared. All seemed to be going smoothly, and I began to dream again of the day when the magazine would be debt-free. Then Hugh's accountants examined our financial records and the deal got cool. After many further drives to Nevada, it became clear that Hugh Roy Marshal was not going to be our white knight.

That attempt had failed, but other options were open. We decided to pursue venture capitalists. This was the mid-1990s, and investors were throwing money at anything that moved and had an Internet component. Thanks to Mike Gorman's brilliant efforts, we had a great website. Bill, Jerry, and I rallied in our attempts to find venture capitalist money. We found the Accelerator group, who had formed to find venture capitalists for needy companies such as ours. They only got shares in the company if a venture capital deal was put together. We began to travel down to San Francisco in an attempt at courting venture capitalists. We went to Scotch-tasting parties, elegant sit-down dinners, pool parties, you name it. But an 18-year-old New Age magazine with a nice website but a large debt was not what the venture capitalists really wanted. So after many months of effort, that option disappeared as well.

The next step involved writing letters and making phone calls to anyone we had ever interviewed or who had written articles for us or we had met or heard of that we thought might have money. We were asking for investment capital and offered limited partner-

ships. We even contacted other magazines and publishing con-
glomerates. People were so nice and sweet—they offered us love
and prayers and all kinds of goodwill. However, no one was willing
to invest. We wrote a comprehensive business plan and hired a
broker to see if anyone wanted to buy the magazine outright. He
eventually found a radio celebrity who said he would buy it for the
debt but not a penny more. Part of the offer was that Jerry and I
would have to walk away and give him the rights to everything that
we had ever printed. Jerry was very tempted to take this offer, but
I was dead-set against it. We argued and finally agreed to refuse. It
felt good to still have control over *Magical Blend*, but that wouldn't
help us remain solvent for much longer.

Now we were all quite depressed, mainly because we didn't see
any way we would have enough money to print issue #53. We
couldn't make payments on our credit cards and lines of credit.
Once you do that for three months, all sorts of bells and whistles
go off at the credit bureaus, not to mention that the late fees,
interest payments, and penalties start stacking up algebraically.
Our printer agreed to put out the issue despite our large debt to
him. In that issue, I wrote an editorial explaining that we were in
dire financial trouble and that unless someone stepped up to
help, that this could be the last issue of *Magical Blend*. Some subscribers sent small checks. A few people called to ask about our
investment guarantees. We couldn't give any.

The debt had grown to a level at which we could no longer pay
the interest, much less the principal. We felt we had only one
option left. Jerry, Bill, and I found a good bankruptcy lawyer and
began the proceedings that we had dreaded for so long. We called
the staff together in December and told them that we were closing
down and that they were all laid off. We paid the little people and
businesses who had always helped us and worked with us and we
informed the printers, credit card companies, and nasty businesses that were chasing after us that we had filed for bankruptcy.

I began applying for positions in Sacramento as a supervisor and manager. I received a few job offers that paid more than I had been making, but they were all middle management jobs in businesses that I didn't really care about. The prospect broke my heart. Meanwhile, we faced our deepest fears of failure as our lawyer led us through the painful process of putting all the financial statements in order. Jerry was devastated and said that he was glad it had come to an end. I felt differently. When our lawyer looked at all our financials, he informed me that if we had a plan to reconfigure the business and go forward as a slimmer organization, then the bankruptcy judge might allow us to sell the magazine cheap to a new owner. That wasn't much consolation at the time, but his words stuck in my mind.

My father felt bad for me and paid for a round-trip ticket so that I could visit him in Florida for a week. I reflected and prayed for guidance. Bankruptcy had always been a big fear with me. Yet if anything, I was persistent. My father felt bad for me but advised me not to continue pursuing projects that weren't sure money-makers. (I loved my Dad, but we didn't always agree. Hearing his advice only strengthened my resolve.) When I returned to Chico, I took Jerry out to breakfast. I told him that I wanted to try one last time. He nearly choked on his orange juice.

"No! No more! We are all done," he practically shouted. I was calm. He and I had been here before; this time I had a different plan. I told him that if he still felt set against continuing, he could sell his half of *Magical Blend* to MB Media, the new company I was about to form. We cut a deal. He would be the freelance editor and write one feature story each issue for six months or until we stopped printing again, whichever came first. I would pay him his old salary and he would be liable for none of the debt I incurred. He was sure this attempt would fail again without him, but he was a true gentleman about it all. If I managed to sell it in the next two years, I agreed to give him half of any profit. We went to court and presented the new reorganization plan to the bankruptcy judge. The deal called for me to take much less pay for the first six months, rehire far fewer staff members than before, and print slimmer magazines with less color. The judge signed off on the plan, and we walked away from huge printer and credit card debt.

This was the most exquisitely painful experience in my entire career. Bankruptcy tore at my soul, forcing me to confront demons of powerlessness and failure that I had always feared. But in the end, the system worked for us, allowing me and *Magical Blend* to start over fresh, without debts or partners. Once we got the approval from the judge, I called up and rehired Victor and Rene. Allen Payne, Michelle Olson, and Mara Benson also came aboard to help us sell ads and run the office. We spent our first three days together reexamining everything and deciding how to improve everything about the business, with an eye toward increased profits and efficiency, all without losing our initial intent, integrity, and vision.

Jerry and I kept to our deal. Six months after we got back into business, he was ready to give up editorial responsibilities for *Magical Blend.* I remember our last conversation on that day. I said to Jerry, "I hope that after a while, we can become friends separate from the magazine."

Jerry thought for a moment and replied, "Michael, I think that we have done everything we were meant to do together. Our karma is very much done. I don't think we should be friends or even acknowledge each other if we meet again. I don't hate you, but we have just shared too much and now it's very over." He was true to his word.

I had neither seen nor heard from him in six years. But then my friend and editor Frank DeMarco insisted that I approach Jerry to credit him and his role in this book and the story of *Magical Blend* magazine. He and his lover are living in Missouri, where Jerry does freelance editing. His health is still not great, but as always, Jerry was polite. He stated, "I can forgive most things that transpired between us, but I never could have forgiven you if you had published a book about the history of *Magical Blend* and didn't use my name." We talked for a long time and agreed to slowly explore reestablishing communications and eventually being friends once more. If this book does nothing else, that conversation was a huge healing for me.

Miracles on Main Street

In 1998 the bankruptcy cleared and I hired back most of the staff. Michelle Olson supervised the ad sales and distribution. With Jerry stepping out, I became the managing editor. Mara handled a wide array of income, subscriber, and organizational tasks. Allen Payne and Victor Cantu were my advertising department, and Rene worked hard to redesign the magazine's layouts so that they would feel more mainstream. I brought on two eager interns, and the three of us (with input from the rest of the staff) repositioned the magazine's editorial content. My days were split between meetings with staff members, going over financials, and most joyously reading editorial submissions, editing, and writing. This last role was one that I had never played before, but after Jerry's departure I had to assume more editorial responsibility. I only did this for a year, because I could hire people to do editorial better than me, but finding good supervisors was more difficult. I did savor that year as managing editor and the fact that sales skyrocketed made me feel great!

It was during this time that I began breaking our ties with many contributing writers that we had worked with for years. I called them all and said that we couldn't pay any writers for the foreseeable future while we emerged from bankruptcy. If they were still interested in working for us, I told them about how we were working to reposition the editorial with greater mainstream appeal. If that didn't scare them off (along with the fact that I was now in charge of editorial decisions instead of Jerry), I told them to submit something and we would see. Sirona Knight was one of the few former regular writers who adapted well to our new editorial format.

It was during this time that John Osborne, who had acquired his Ph.D. from the California Institute of Integral Studies and taught English at Butte Community College, started writing for us. His regular articles were a wonderful introduction to spirituality for many of our readers, and John has continued to contribute to *Magical Blend* for the last several years.

Around then, I read a small article about the Internet and its possibilities in *The Synthesis,* a local weekly paper. The author was a fellow by the name of Bret Lueder. I called up the newspaper's owner, who was a friend, and asked him how to get in touch with the writer. Bret ended up writing a great piece for us, and has been a regular contributor and member of the extended *Magical Blend* family ever since.

In the year following our emergence from bankruptcy, we made the conscious decision to reposition *Magical Blend* more toward the mainstream. Our new issues would feature more travel, more alternative health, more music, and more of what we like to call "Miracles on Main Street." For quite some time, I had felt that our esoteric, intellectual, and occasionally occult-based content had reached the limit of its potential readership. By the time we emerged from the bankruptcy, it seemed that many of those readers no longer needed us. Yet there was a void in our society, and it was found within people who were just opening up to nondenominational spiritual growth and methods of self-improvement, yet who had no community or support system, and no dependable place to explore possibilities. It was to this ever-growing potential audience that we now aimed our magazine.

Wow, did we ever guess right! The response was fantastic, sales were steady, and income started accruing in the place of debt. Everyone, it seemed, had been talking about *Magical Blend*'s desperation, bankruptcy, and unavoidably sad ending. But we re-emerged as a new and different magazine, one that was still aligned with our original intentions and vision, just updated for a new world. The response was a wonderful confirmation that adaptation is the key to success in any endeavor.

Once the office got going again it became obvious that without Jerry Snider or Bill Hall, I needed someone else to assist in management and planning. Michelle Olson had started with us selling classified ads on a part-time basis. Then she had moved onto our distribution department, helping subscription growth as well as wholesaler and retailer sales. From there, she helped refine our website, bringing in more money through the Internet than anyone at *Magical Blend,* either before or since. Then she had switched back to selling display ads full time and did very well working with or against the territorial but superb sales team of Victor and Allen.

Michelle was young, energetic, inventive, and a good businessperson; everyone liked her immensely. So Mara, our office manager, suggested that I should promote Michelle to the position of general manager. I asked the rest of the staff, some friends, and a few psychics. They all agreed.

Promoting Michelle made the next 18 months a pleasure. With her friendship and great insights we were able to stabilize the new format. We increased circulation and improved most aspects of the magazine. As a natural consequence, our finances improved.

Meanwhile, we hired two highly qualified and motivated editors, who were revamping editorial after Jerry's departure. I gave them more say and I moved back to planning and choosing one or two articles and vetoing the ones I didn't like. Mara and Allen became involved in editorial as well, specifically working with the many great musical artists that had appeal to our readership. Between them, Mara and Allen got us terrific interviews with fascinating folks like Tori Amos, Ritchie Blackmore, and Santana.

Jim Self and Roxanne Barrett, who operated the Avalon Psychic Institute in Chico (now in Truckee, California), had read my editorial pleading for assistance during our troubled times. They unselfishly volunteered to help by giving us a free course in business intuition and spiritual operations. Their weekly sessions greatly assisted us in realigning and refining our renewed vision of success and spiritual growth.

Everything worked well until the summer of 2000. At that point, I was scheduled to take a two-and-a-half-week vacation to New England with my family to visit our extended families. Three weeks before my departure, Michelle and I sat down. She had been running her own sign-making business on nights and weekends for the better part of a year. The business was growing fast and she had begun making more money doing that than working at *Magical Blend*, even though she had to work much harder for us. She asked what I could do to help ease this unbalance. Our finances were good but not fantastic. I made her an offer, but it wasn't what she wanted or felt she deserved. Michelle was hurt and very disappointed. Yet she loved *Magical Blend* and was very loyal to me. She was also torn. Her business was doing well and demanding all of her free time. She had made such great decisions for so long that I didn't realize that after that meeting, she had begun to pull away.

When I got back to the office three weeks later, Michelle gave her notice. The staff dynamic had melted down while I was away. Some of the newer staff came to the conclusion that Michelle and I were getting paid too much and they not enough. They even concocted a scenario in which I was skimming off the real profits and investing them in comic books. So, soon after Michelle's resignation, we had more staff turnovers.

To fill in the gaps, we hired Harriet Chrisna and Syd Robinson to handle editorial, and brought in Danny Liend to run the office. Dawn Ginn came on in the ad sales department and proved through her persistence that health food and health companies of all sorts could do well advertising in *Magical Blend*. Dawn Ginn's career with us lasted about one intense year. After helping the magazine expand into the natural health category, Dawn sadly decided to leave and go homestead with her family in Missouri.

I also began planning how and when to replace Michelle.

Without her I made some ambitious and risky expansion decisions and began growing a new debt! When would I ever learn?

That summer, we hired Harry Coyote as an advertising sales representative. He had owned an electric power machine company and oil rig supply company, both of which he had recently sold so that he could spend more time with his wife and grown kids in Chico. Harry certainly didn't need any money, but he took the job with us in order to stay busy. He loved phone sales but got bored easily. He sold well.

We had another great treat that summer when Mike Richman, a very talented writer, editor, and magazine circulation professional, quit his high-paying, high-pressure job in New York City, sold his house and car and moved to Chico in an attempt to find more meaning in life. He had applied for an editing or writing job in August. I made Mike an offer: We would let him write and edit if he would focus mainly on growing our circulation. He agreed and he quickly became an integral part of the team.

As I stated, in the months after Michelle left, I made a series of decisions that, in retrospect, were not very wise. We were really trying to push the envelope and expand our readership wherever possible. In fact, we did achieve some accelerated growth, but it cost us much more than we made. Expensive expansion is easy to do in a small business, and before we knew it, we found ourselves with a debt again by the close of the year. Deanna Leah and Leah McKean had both come aboard by that time. Both of them had great skills and passion for our mission. Rene was running the art department and laying out the magazine with great efficiency and ability. Mike was a big help both in marketing and as our editorial director once Harriet left. But alone I didn't see any of them running the business if I were to take any time off. So, we began to interview candidates for the job of chief operating officer—a position that we had never had before. The ideal person was someone who could run MB Media while I spent more time away from the office, writing and traveling.

Just before the end of 2000, Harry walked into my office and said, "I like what you have built here and somewhat how you run it. What portion of ownership and control would you be willing to give my wife and me if we invested enough to pay off the debt and invest some money in wise growth?" Now I was excited! A man who could sell and who had run his own business profitably wanted to invest in us. We did quite a bit of negotiating, and Mike and Rene helped out with the details. Then we signed a letter of intent to bring Harry in as a partner. So, with every reason to believe that I had handled the debt, I hired Betty Jones to be our first COO. She had an amazing resume and far outshined everyone else we interviewed. Her accounting and business skills alone were awesome and she seemed great in organizing, setting up, and improving systems. Harry, Mike, and Rene all thought that she was great as well. After some more detailed negotiations, we had a deal. Betty came aboard officially that April. On the same day, Susan Dobra appeared in our midst. Susan is a Ph.D. who was then teaching philosophy at Chico State University. She had loved *Magical Blend* for years and was interested in volunteering to assist with editorial.

The strangest hire I ever had might have been Claudia Cuentas. One day around this time, a beautiful young lady walked up our stairs and asked if she could speak with the publisher. I wasn't too overwhelmed that day, so I said sure. We sat down and she immediately said, "I think I am supposed to be working here."

I asked if she had ever worked on a magazine. No. Sold advertising? No. Sold anything? Not really. Done much office work? No. Any good at filing or data entry? Only so-so. We weren't getting anyplace, so I asked her to tell me a little about herself.

"Well," she said, "I am a student at Chico State, majoring in music and education. I love to dance and I grew up in Lima, Peru."

"I do love Peru," I replied. "But that doesn't qualify you to work here."

Claudia thought about this for a moment. "I know some of your employees, and I have read some of your magazines. Also, I have been taking a course at the Avalon Psychic Institute and I just feel intuitively that I am supposed to work here."

She seemed to have some real passion for our mission, so I took a chance. "I am about to leave town for the next two weeks," I informed her. "I like your energy. If you have any more insights about what it is you are supposed to do, come back after my return and let me know. I will give it some thought as well."

I actually didn't give it all that much thought, and had in fact all but forgotten about this incident when she showed up two weeks and three days later. She said, "I came back because I still feel strongly that I am meant to work here. But I am no clearer on what I am supposed to do."

I had no idea either, but I was impressed by her persistence. It turned out that we had a bunch of small projects that needed doing and didn't require much experience; however, everyone else was too busy to get to them. So I said, "OK, Claudia, we will give you two weeks of part-time work and see what comes of it."

She accomplished everything we gave her with flair, quality, and enthusiasm. She shone light and joy throughout the office, and when her two weeks were up, we agreed that she could have a part-time job filling in on whatever projects needed attention. When there was nothing much else to do, she also tried her hand at selling ads. Of course, she turned out to be a great ad salesperson because everyone she talked to felt her enthusiasm. She brought her radiant energy into the office for about a year, then one day it ended much as it began.

Claudia came into my office and said, "It is time for me to leave the staff. I have really learned lots working here and love most everyone here. I have been offered a paid student teacher position and I need the credits to graduate. So this is my last week. But we will stay friends, right Michael?"

"Of course we will, Claudia," I replied.

When most staff leave on good terms, they usually say something like this, and I end up hearing from them every once in a great while. Claudia has been one of the rare exceptions. She has stayed close to my whole family. We have visited her and her family in Peru. She comes to our house for dinner every now and then. She has tutored me in Spanish. She even organized all the great music we had at my last book release party.

By May, Allen Payne was uncomfortable with all the changes. After a great and enjoyable tenure with *Magical Blend*, he applied for and got a better paying job selling cable television. Harry's money was slow in arriving, but I had let him take over the ad department and have a say in all other key decisions. Our bills, especially the ones with our printer, were again way overdue and we were all a bit weirded out. I began pressuring Harry for the money and he stopped coming to work. Then he had his phone disconnected and moved. I never figured out if he got cold feet, changed his mind, or was just playing a very strange game, but here it was the month of May and we had a growing debt again, which frightened me. Plus, we had lost two great ad salespeople and revenues were slow. I began to freak out and panic, but Betty, Mike, and Rene convinced me that if we made adjustments and kept our belts tight, then we would get out of debt.

We had an all-staff meeting, in which I tearfully informed the staff that we were deep in debt and that I couldn't make payroll. I told them that I was unclear when we would be able to pay them for their last two weeks of salary, and that for the foreseeable future we wouldn't be able to pay any hourly wages or salaries whatsoever. I suggested that anyone who wanted to continue working for MB Media under these circumstances would have to figure how to make it on a commission-only basis, for work performed that brought in trackable income. These personal proposals could be presented to me, and everyone else was to apply for unemployment right away.

The entire staff thanked me, reassured me, and returned to their desks to work even more diligently than before. They refused to accept leaving, even though we couldn't pay them. Over the next few days, I sat down with every staff member to discuss how they could alter their role or expand their job description to generate more income for the business as well as make enough commission to make ends meet for themselves. I was so very touched and honored by this amazing testimony to how much the staff believed in what we were doing.

The changes that we implemented afterward made major differences. The whole staff was dedicated and determined to turn the debt around and we did. Things stabilized through the summer and then slowly, we began to create a positive cash flow. We eventually paid off the debt in full; furthermore, we felt comfortable enough to launch our second magazine, *Natural Beauty & Health,* that August. It has been a wonderful success that has added a great deal to our company.

As things improved, and Betty, Mike, and Rene assumed greater roles in decision making, I began to turn my attention toward manifesting the second part of a plan that had been revealed to me by the Inca goddesses and gods many years before. Traveling to Peru was a dream that was very important to Deborah, the kids, and me. When we adopted Henry and Sophia, we had made a promise to them and to ourselves that we would one day return as a family to live in Peru for a significant period of time before they were teenagers. By the summer of 2001, both of them were nearly teenagers. Deborah and I realized that if we were going to keep our promise, it had better happen soon. She had an opportunity to take a sabbatical from September through December from her job at Chico State University. I began sending sample chapters and proposals to publishers for a book I had always want to write on Peru and the lost spiritual teachings of the Incas. Deborah got her sabbatical approved and I received an advance from Career Press/New Pages Books on my Peru project. Now I just had to worry about the magazine's ability to survive without me for four months.

When I left in September we had Victor, Deanna, Leah,

Claudia, Michael Aaron Liddle, Tom Rider, and Brandon Vasquez selling advertising. Betty, Mike, Rene, and Susan had the operations and production side of things down. We had the lovely and inspired Amanda Bush and Laura Smailes doing office work and filling in where needed. We had seldom had so many quality professionals in so many key roles. It was wonderful! The day before my departure the staff had a going away gathering for me. I looked around at this staff, and I was filled with pride at having gathered such a great group together. I was sure that I could trust them and they could handle whatever came up in my absence. I gave thanks for all of them and felt very blessed. I left for my grand excursion early in September of 2001, full of optimism and hope for the future.

All of us know what happened next. My family and I were in Lima, Peru, when the world changed on 9/11. I stayed in close e-mail contact with the office over the next few weeks. Advertising sales—most revenues, in fact—slowed to a trickle, and the so-called "sacred travel" companies stopped buying ads altogether. Many of these advertisers had been with us for years and we had come to count on their ad dollars. Fearing the worst, I told Betty, Mike, and Rene that if business just came to a complete halt they would have to lay off the staff and close the office until I returned. But Betty, Mike, and Rene were fighters; more than that, they were dedicated professionals who knew how to handle the tough times. They tightened the belt as far as it would go, only spending money on what was absolutely necessary. They were forced to lay off a few staff members, and they sure couldn't hire any new ones, but somehow they kept the doors open. It was only later that I realized they had lent the business significant amounts of their own money to cover payroll and printer bills. They held MB Media and *Magical Blend* together in those very dark days.

Whatever happened, I was determined to have a great trip in Peru, and we did. However, by December ad sales were almost nonexistent and income was very slow. When I got home, Betty made it clear that the business needed me to be Neal Powers, the ad sales maniac and head cheerleader. Victor, Claudia, Michael Aaron, Tom, and Brandon were all quite discouraged and each left not long after my return. Victor went on to sell ads for a different magazine, while Michael Aaron became a Reiki healer, Brandon graduated college and got a job in marketing down in Southern California, and Tom opened his own restaurant right here in Chico. He named it Oberon's, and the food is great. I hear it is doing very well.

We made Deanna the new advertising sales manager and she, along with Leah and myself, began interviewing new sales applicants. We found Stephen Morgenstern, who had sold insurance and was looking for a challenging job with more meaning. Over the next few months we added Janie, Joan, and Ashley, all of whom became solid salespeople for us. As time went along, the dynamic continued to change. Mike Richman left for a personal vision quest, and Susan became our managing editor. Then, Betty left, Mike returned in the capacity of operations director, and we hired the great Paul Stevens as our current COO.

Today, in 2004, no day at MB Media seems average. However, most days (as I finish writing this book) go something like this:

I usually drop my children off at high school and arrive at the MB Media office by 8 A.M. Paul is always here to greet me, since he arrives every morning at 6 A.M. or earlier. Kathy Hawthorne, our office manager who we welcomed back in 2002, is usually there by 7:30 A.M. Rene, my always dependable art director, usually arrives about the same time as I, and on Mondays, Wednesdays, and Fridays, his 18-year-old son, Randy, comes with him. Randy manages our online eBay store and generally assists Rene. They are quickly followed by Izumi, our talented webmaster. We take turns making the coffee. Members of the ad sales staff can arrive any time between 5 A.M. and 9 A.M. Most of the rest of the staff come in at 9 A.M. except for Susan and Mike, both of whom arrive about 10 A.M. and work deep into the evening.

After coffee, I check my e-mail while Paul debriefs me on the day's plans and goals. These can vary in the extreme. I might be meeting with editorial to make decisions on future issues. We usually have ten issues planned ahead. However, we are always tweaking and modifying one detail or another until we send them to the printer. I often meet with advertising to troubleshoot ideas on landing and maintaining big accounts and how we can best serve the needs of our readers and advertisers. Paul and I go over cash flow, ad sales performance, distribution figures, and plans for growth on a daily basis. I will meet with Rene to brainstorm about cover designs, to sign off on layouts, or to discuss technical needs or problems. Mike often acts as our unofficial personnel director and brings me up to date on personnel needs, concerns, or problems, which often result in my meeting with one of the ad sales executives or our part-time database manager and computer programmer, Eric. Also, I meet with Izumi about web and Internet developments.

In the summer, I usually bring a salad from our garden at home for lunch; in the winter, it's a bowl of soup from vegetables we have frozen from our garden. One or two days a week I will go out to eat alone, or with a member of the staff or another friend. Paul leaves about two in the afternoon. I am usually able to read some rough edits of articles we are considering, or do some writing on my editorial or some other piece. I attempt to stay on top of my public relations activities, making sure to apply to speak at certain conferences, setting up radio and TV interviews, and deciding when and where to offer workshops. My children walk to the office from school, and if they don't have sports practice, they usually arrive by three-thirty. They find an empty desk and do their homework until it's time to leave. When they are on traveling sports teams such as soccer, tennis, or baseball, I might have to transport them to practice at any time between three and six. Then I usually work in the office until they are done and pick them up and head home.

We've obviously changed a great deal, even in the years follow-ing our tumultuous bankruptcy. After turning over most of our sales staff in the middle of 2003, MB Media emerged as a leaner organization, still balancing on that razor's edge between making money and making a difference in the world. And so here we are today.

Flexibility and Adaptation

Before I left for my Peruvian trip in 2001, I looked closely at our office as well as the staff. The office is "bare bones." It's not fancy—*Magical Blend* has never had a fancy office. It's a comfort-able, serviceable place with lots of room and, in recent years, an awareness of feng shui. The richest spot has an altar to our suc-cess. There's lots of "up" energy, but not too much storage. We have reconfigured the rooms an endless number of times; I have personally worked at every single desk and computer terminal in the place.

To me, our office reflects some of the essence of what *Magical Blend* has been over the span of its 25-year history. Few if any of us have ever been caught up in material things. We believe in who we are and what we do for a living. We usually trust each other to do what's right for the business, our readers, and our working part-ners. And we stay flexible at all times, because life on a razor's edge is many things, but complacent is not one of them.

The mature years of *Magical Blend* drove that lesson home in spades. I didn't plan for the entire company to abandon the Bay Area and move to Chico. I didn't plan to have major chest surgery, or go bankrupt, or part ways with some of my longest-lasting friends, comrades, and business associates. I certainly didn't plan for the world to fall apart in the aftermath of 9/11. However, these things all happened, and we adjusted and moved forward better than before.

I have taken to referring to myself and MB Media as the "Masters of Change." I like that. It makes me feel somewhat in control of the chaos that sometimes (OK, usually) swirls around the office. But it's more than that. It's been said that all living things must adapt to survive. As you can probably tell by now, I think of *Magical Blend* and *Natural Beauty & Health* as living entities. And yes, they have adapted and changed radically over the years. Sometimes, just for fun, I look back at a copy of issue #1 and marvel at who we were then, and what we have become. Maria Nuez, Jerry Snider, Carmen Lorata, William Stewart, Joe Blondo, and the rest were my compatriots in those days, as are Paul Stevens, Rene Schmidt, Mike Richman, and Susan Dobra now. There was a sense of exuberance and optimism in those early days that I miss sometimes, but it's wonderful to walk the halls of our office today and revel in the professionalism and dedication that everyone here still shares. MB Media is special, sacred, and, yes, ever changing. That's what makes it all so fascinating.

Twenty-five years is a long time for anyone to devote to a project, especially one with the magnitude and scope of *Magical Blend*. Yet I feel as energized and excited as ever. Yes, it's been a long, strange trip, but it's something that I wouldn't have done any other way. The past is what it is; the future will be what it will be. But for now, today, I can say without question that I am enormously proud of what we've built here at MB Media. We have made an impact on the lives of literally millions of people over the years, affecting the way in which they view themselves and their unrealized potential. I couldn't have done it any other way. Being a part of *Magical Blend* is a dream that has come true, and keeps coming true, every single day. What can I say? I'm blessed to have had the opportunity to follow my heart and make a living out of it. And if you ever get the chance to follow your own heart and start a business that you love, my advice would simply be: Do it! Make your dreams into reality, and you'll never have to work another day in your life.

A MAGICAL FUTURE

At the beginning of this book, I stated my belief that all beings on planet Earth now stand at the crossroads. Over the next decade, we will set the path for the spiritual evolution not only of humanity, but for most other species who exist on our planet. *Magical Blend* magazine will not tip the scales by itself. Neither will *Natural Beauty & Health,* MB Media, or Michael Peter Langevin— no one organization, magazine, business, or individual can make the difference alone. But together we can cocreate our greatest possible future, one that is magical and fulfilling.

I wrote this story at this time in large part because my publisher, editor, and friend, Frank DeMarco, encouraged and indulged me. This project has helped me greatly in reviewing *Magical Blend's* evolution. For that I will always be grateful. But there is more to it than that. I view the history of *Magical Blend* as a parable.

Magical Blend has often been compared to a compost heap. While that doesn't sound like much of a compliment, in truth it is. The way in which our magazine functions as a business, how issues come together, our physical space, and even the status of my desk is usually messy, sometimes smelly, occasionally even repugnant. It's hard to get a fix on the process when you view it close up. However, like a compost heap, what we finally end up publishing in an issue are the riches of fertile loams. We have printed nearly 100 issues. In each one we attempted to use words and images to explore and share glimpses into the essence of spirituality and the expanded, often unseeable and undefinable, multidimensional nature of our universe.

Our story portrays the determination to publish a successful, unique, ever-evolving, and transformative magazine despite many obstacles, setbacks, and defeats. Time and again we had to face our fears and embrace our hopes, all the while continuing to distribute information that inspires, stretches, uplifts, and enhances the lives of those who read it. Ours has been the archetypical hero's journey, with the hero being *Magical Blend* itself.

We have always been an underpaid, ragtag staff of rebels, misfits, and people attempting to get their lives back together or trying to achieve their ambitions. Seldom have the members of the staff shared many common values or goals beyond doing their assigned job and whatever else they could to assist in producing and distributing the highest quality magazines possible. The cast of characters has changed and evolved; some stayed longer and provided stability and vision. Others came in, contributed, and left in days, weeks, months, or even a few years. All left having added to what *Magical Blend* is and having been personally altered by the experience.

As I finish this book, we are preparing the next issue of *Magical Blend.* The theme is predictions and prophecies. I must admit that although I have read more of that kind of material than most people, I can't even guess at what most of the details of our shared future will bring. The past was predicted based on spiritual hopes. Life was historically so very difficult that the only hope was a Utopian future world or for a paradise in the afterlife. The case can be made that many of history's greatest prophets gave us moral codes in the forms of religions, with themselves as father figures assisting humanity in improving their daily existence. In the last two or three hundred years, you could fairly claim that the majority of our world has embraced capitalism and science as our new religions. These have been embraced on a wide scale, altering the prophecies of the past and transforming our dreamed-of future into something more like a technological Utopia. I do not claim to know what our future holds, any more than I can say that time travel will become a reality or how it will function.

What I do know is very simple: We each have control of this present moment—how we embrace it, how we use it, and how we react to outside stimuli. No one can convince me that my thoughts, words, or deeds are predestined; guided by destiny, perhaps, but I believe that we all have free will. If this is so, then we can affect the future. We can dedicate as many thoughts, words, and deeds towards actions that will make the world a better place, whether that is as simple as being a little nicer to each other or getting more involved in community service. I feel my efforts with our publications contribute to a better tomorrow. Beyond that, we all affect the children who are the living incarnation of the future. I believe every positive, loving, learning experience that I share with my children and their friends are actions towards building the future of my dreams. As always, I urge all of you to be mindful of the present moments of your life and fill them with loving actions. But most of all, let's help our children know that they are loved and help them to fulfill their highest potential, for only then will we guarantee our best possible future.

We can make our future positive, but only if we choose to do so and hold the unshakeable belief in our own power of manifestation. The coming decade is our great time of decision.

Everything that we do will contribute to the outcome of whether we, our children, our children's children, and their children shall live in a Golden Age or a much less desirable alternative. Please take from this book whatever you can and enjoy every moment we have to experience the miracle of human life. Keep the hope and dream of magic alive in your heart, and thus it shall never perish from the Earth. Thanks for sharing the *Magical Blend* journey!

ABOUT THE AUTHOR

Michael Peter Langevin is now and has been for 25 years the publisher/managing editor of MB Media which produces *Magical Blend, Natural Beauty & Health,* and *Transitions.* For most of that time, his editorials have been the first writing to appear in each issue. Each of these magazines has recently surpassed 120,000 in circulation. They are sold in all major chain stores in the U.S. and in 33 other countries. He lectures, teaches classes, and does workshops regularly from coast to coast.

Michael Peter was the host of *Magical Blend* TV show for two years in San Francisco and has appeared on TV and radio often. His book, *Secrets of the Ancient Incas,* was released in 2002 and was well received. He edited and contributed to several anthologies, including *Solstice Shift* and *A Magical Universe.*

When not traveling, leading workshops, or managing MB Media, he resides with his family, horses, and dogs on a farm in the foothills of the Sierra Nevada Mountains. To reach Michael Peter, sign up for a workshop, buy back issues, or subscribe to *Magical Blend,* visit online at www.magicalblend.com.

Hampton Roads Publishing Company

. . . for the evolving human spirit

Hampton Roads Publishing Company
publishes books on a variety of subjects,
including metaphysics, health,
visionary fiction, and other related topics.

For a copy of our latest catalog, call toll-free
(800) 766-8009, or send your name and address to:

Hampton Roads Publishing Company, Inc.
1125 Stoney Ridge Road
Charlottesville, VA 22902

e-mail: hrpc@hrpub.com
www.hrpub.com